Spoken English

Published by :
Lotus Press Publishers & Distributors

Spoken English

A detailed and simplified course for learning Spoken English

Namrata Palta

Lotus
PRESS
4735/22, Prakash Deep Building,
Ansari Road, Daryaganj,
New Delhi - 110002

Lotus Press : Publishers & Distributors
Unit No. 220, 2nd Floor, 4735/22, Prakash Deep Building,
Ansari Road, Darya Ganj, New Delhi- 110002
Ph.: 23280047, 98118-38000
• E-mail : lotuspress1984@gmail.com
www.lotuspress.co.in

Spoken English

ISBN: 81-8382-052-2

Printed & Published by : **Lotus Press Publishers & Distributors,** New Delhi-02

CONTENTS

INTRODUCTION

To the Student

This book is designed to help you master your concepts in English and become friendly with the grammar and rules you need to be familiar with.

You may use this book for self-study and practice along with it.

Consider this

English has become a mandatory requirement in today's world. People who have good English get jobs more easily as compared to non-speakers.

It is therefore important to start today and create globally understandable English so that we can converse easily with global customers.

Every sound of every language is within every child, but as we grow, we stop listening to different sounds, and get enveloped in our comfort zone and stop listening to the sounds that we have never heard. If you walk down the street you may notice that people speak English differently. The reason why they sound different is because every individual has a different cultural background.

To remove this we have built four different sections in this book to overall develop your grammar, pronunciation and vocabulary along with your conversational skills.

A FEW TIPS ON HOW TO USE THIS BOOK:

ü Divide your sections month-wise.

ü Give each section a time of one month to master.

ü Pick up the content from the book and then revise what you have learnt on a daily basis.

ü Read aloud in English atleast twice a day.

ü Till you are learning from this book, focus on listening to English news channels and movie channels.

ü Use your dictionary. Become familiar with the phonetic symbols of your dictionary.

ü Make a list of frequently used words that are difficult for you to pronounce and verify how a native speaker pronounces them.

ü Record yourself reading some sections of a book.

ü Pronounce the endings of each word. Pay special stress to "s" and "ed" endings.

ü Be Patient—You can change the way you speak but it won't happen overnight!

ü Speak with more energy and enthusiasm.

Always Remember

"It's not what you say but how you say it that counts"

SECTION 1—PRONUNCIATION BUILDER–PHONETICS

Pronouncing the Alphabets

A	AEY
B	BEE
C	SEE
D	DHI
E	IEE
F	EHF
G	GEE
H	AITCH
I	AYE
J	JHAY
K	KHAY
L	ELLE
M	EMME
N	ENNE
O	OHH
P	PHI
Q	QUEUE
R	ARE
S	ESS
T	THI
U	YOU
V	WE

W	**DUBYU**
X	**EX**
Y	**WHY**
Z	**ZEE**

Pronouncing the Months

January-***Jan-u-ree***	October-***ok-toe-ber***
February-***Feb-u-ree***	November-***no-vem-ber***
March-***Ma-ar-ch (ch as in 'child')***	December-***dis-ember***
April-***Ape-rell (rhyme with 'well')***	
May-***Meh***	
June-***Joon***	
July-***Joo-lie***	
August-***Aww-gust (rhyme with 'must')***	
September-***sep-tem-ber***	

Consonant Sounds

To begin with consonant sounds you need to remember that there are 5 vowels (a, e, I, o, u) in English language and the rest 21 alphabets are consonants.

It has been noticed that we usually sound low on enthusiasm because of the lack of knowledge of the consonant sound. Also, the non-clarity of the consonant makes us pronounce the word incorrectly.

TWO COMMON PROBLEMS FACED WHILE PRONOUNCING CONSONANTS:

✓ **S/SH**- Due to this problem we are not able to differentiate between words with 's' sound and words with 'sh' sound.

Example: SHE SEA

SHE-To say this throw out air outside and the tongue should be behind your teeth touching the front set of teeth.

SEA-To say this pull in your tongue and take the air inside. The tongue should be pulled inside and should not touch the front teeth.

PRACTICE THIS:	She	sells	seashells	on the	seashore.
	(Sh)	(s)	(S) (Sh)		(s) (Sh)

✓ **Z/ZH**- In this we are not able to pronounce the sounds Z and Zh differently.

Example:

ZH	Z
Measure	Zoo
Pleasure	Prize
Treasure	Exams
Azure	Exist

For ZH air has to be pulled into the mouth without opening the teeth.

For Z air has to be thrown out and tongue has to be between the teeth.

Practicing all the Consonants

Now, let us practice each consonant and the sound related to it. After, you learn the sound practice saying it aloud.

Practicing the Consonant 

Background

✓ Most often the /b/ sound in the initial, final, and medial positions is made by the consonant *b* as it is represented in words such as *bat, tab,* and *number.*

1. Initial-(letter 'b' as the first alphabet)-Bat
2. Medial-(letter 'b' as the middle alphabet)-

   Number
3. Final-(letter 'b' as the last alphabet)-Tab

✓ The use of the consonant *b* is very consistent-it only makes this one sound-**'Bbbb'**

✓ When *b* is doubled, one *b* is silent, such as in *blubber.*

✓ It is also silent when it follows *m* in one-syllable words such as *limb, comb,* and *tomb,* as well as when it precedes *t* in words like *doubt* and *debt.*

PRACTICE THIS

The big bumblebee slept in the barn on a blue bed, and when it awoke it buzzed by the bump on my head.

Other words you can use:

/b/ -at

/b/ -ird

/b/ -ed

/b/ -one

/b/ -ook

Practicing the Consonant 

Background

- ✓ The letter *c* is not a reliable letter in terms of the sound it makes because it can represent so many different sounds.
- ✓ It makes both a ***hard and soft sound.***
- ✓ The ***hard /k/*** as represented in the words ***cat*** and ***cake*** is the most common pronunciation.
- ✓ The hard sound is usually made by *c* when it precedes the **vowels *a, o,* or *u*.**
- ✓ The letter *c* is also usually hard when followed by a consonant, as in the ***cl*** and ***cr*** in the words ***clam*** and ***cream***.
- ✓ The letter *c* makes a **soft sound like /s/ when followed by *i* (*circus, circle, cigar*), *y* (*cycle, cyst*), and *e* (*center, cell, cereal*).**
- ✓ It is also usually soft in the final position when followed by silent *e (race, nice)*.
- ✓ The *c* is sometimes **both hard and soft** when doubled in words like ***succeed***.
- ✓ When doubled in words like *occupy,* one *c* is silent.
- ✓ If *c* comes before *e* or *i,* it can make a /sh/ sound, as in words like *ocean, racial,* and *social*.

Practicing the Consonant 

Background

- ✓ Most often, the /d/ sound in the initial, final, and medial positions is made by the consonant *d* as it is represented in words such as *desk, bed,* and *middle*.

- ✓ The use of the consonant *d* is very consistent - it only makes this one sound.
- ✓ However, when *d* is doubled, one *d* is silent, as in *fiddle.*
- ✓ It can also be pronounced /t/ as in the words *tipped, mopped,* and *hoped.*
- ✓ Other spellings of the /d/ sound include *ed* as in *voted* and *wanted, t* as in *water, tt* as in *butter* and *mutter,* and *ld* as in *should* and *would.*

PRACTICE THIS

Dan the duck paddled in the muddy pond as Danny Deer danced and fiddled the day away.

She climbed out drenched and dripping on the deck.

Practicing the Consonant 

Background

- ✓ Most often, the /f/ sound in the initial, final, and medial positions is made by the consonant *f* as it is represented in words such as *fat, if,* and *often.*
- ✓ The use of the consonant *f* is very consistent for it only makes this one sound.
- ✓ When *f* is doubled, as in *off,* one *f* is silent.
- ✓ The sound /f/ is also represented by the digraphs *ph*, as in *phone and graph,* and *gh* as in *enough* and *rough*.

PRACTICE THIS

The fast furry fox flew across a field in a flash.

While the frisky frog and fish fell into a pond with a splash.

The fox and the wolf were afraid to jump the fence after each hurt a foot when falling off the cliff.

Practicing the Consonant

Background

- ✓ The letter *g* is not a reliable letter in terms of the sound it makes.

  It makes both a **hard** and **soft** sound.
- ✓ The **hard /g/** as represented in the words ***gate*** and ***go*** is the most common pronunciation.
- ✓ The hard sound is usually made by *g* when it follows the vowels *a, e, i, o,* or *u*.
- ✓ The letter *g* is also usually hard when followed by a consonant, as in the *gl* and *gr* blends.
- ✓ The letter **g makes a soft sound like *j*, when followed by *e (gem)*, *y (gym)*, and *i (giant)*.**
- ✓ It is also usually soft in the medial position and in final position when followed by silent *e (page)*. But there are exceptions: for example, *forget, girl,* and *give*.
- ✓ When *g* is double as in *suggest* the first *g* is hard, and the second *g* is soft.

PRACTICE THIS

The gray goose jumped on the green garden gate on one leg *and gave the good girl a splendid gift of a golden egg.*

The goofy giant gopher gently gave the good gentleman a gift of ginger and gum.

Practicing the Consonant

Background

- ✓ Most often, the /h/ sound in the initial position is made by the consonant *h* as represented in words such as *hat* and *happy*.
- ✓ *H* is not used in the final position and sometimes appears in the medial position in words such as *ahead, ahoy,* and *behave.*
- ✓ The use of the consonant *h* is very consistent because it makes only this one sound.
- ✓ However, when *h* is preceded by *w,* such as in *what* or *when,* the /h/ sound is made before /w/.
- ✓ The sound of h in wh words is silent. This means that the initial sound in *what* is pronounced no differently than the initial sound in *wit* or *wet*.

Practicing the Consonant

Background

- ✓ The letter *j* is not a reliable letter in terms of the sound it makes.

- ✓ The /j/ as represented in the words *jump* and *jug* is the most common pronunciation.
- ✓ *J* is most often in the initial position, sometimes found in the medial position, and seldom in the final position.
- ✓ The /j/ sound is found in spellings other than the letter *j*.

> PRACTICE THIS
>
> ***Jim jumped in a jeep to go get jam and jelly in a jar. While Jeff jogged to a joint for juice instead of driving his junky car.***

Practicing the Consonant 

Background

- ✓ Most often, the /k/ sound in the initial, final, and medial positions is made by the consonant *k* as in *kite, milk,* and *market.* However, in the final and medial positions, the /k/ sound is often written with the letter combination *ck,* as in *quick* and *lucky.*
- ✓ The use of the consonant *k* is consistent for the /k/ sound, although there are other letters and combinations of letters that also make the /k/ sound.
- ✓ Sometimes the consonant *k* is silent, as in the words *know* and *knit.*

Practicing the Consonant 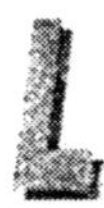

Background

- ✓ The consonant *l* is a reliable letter in that it does not represent any sound other than the /l/ sound in words such as *lip* and *pill.*

- ✓ However, one *l* is silent when it is doubled in words such as *bell* and *hill.*
- ✓ It is also sometimes silent when it comes before letters *k, f, d,* and *m* appearing in the same syllable such as in the words *calf, yolk.*

PRACTICE THIS

Larry liked licking lovely jam on loaves of bread for brunch.

Look, Linda has lettuce leaves and lemons for her lunch.

And for a late dinner it was leg of lamb they liked most to munch.

The frail lion licked its lips when it followed the limping camel into the tall tent.

Practicing the Consonant 

Background

- ✓ Most often the /m/ sound in the initial, medial, and final positions is made by the consonant *m* represented in words such as *map, mother, ham,* and *number.*
- ✓ The use of the consonant *m* is very consistent because it makes only this one sound.
- ✓ However, when *m* is doubled in a word, such as *hammer,* one *m* is silent.
- ✓ There are other spellings of the /m/ sound — for example, *mn* in *hymn* and *mb* in *lamb.*

PRACTICE THIS

My mom makes ham that is so good and so yummy.

I munch my mom's ham until it fills my tummy.

My mother's baked ham smelled mighty amazing and yummy to Jim.

Practicing the Consonant

Background

✓ Most often, the /n/ sound in the initial, final, and medial positions is made by the consonant *n* as in *net, nap, can, fan,* and *ant.*

✓ The use of the consonant *n* is very consistent for the /n/ sound, although there is an exception—the *pn, gn,* and *kn* letter combinations in words like *pneumonia, gnat,* and *know.*

✓ Sometimes the consonant *n* is silent, such as when it is the second *n* in words like *Ann* and *dinner,* or when it follows the letter *m,* as in the word *hymn.*

Practicing the Consonant

Background

✓ Most often, the /p/ sound in the initial, final, and medial positions is made by the consonant *p* as represented by words such as—*pet, tap,* or *ape.*

✓ The use of the consonant *p* is very consistent for this sound, although there is an exception—the *ph* combination in a word like *diphthong.*

- ✓ Sometimes the consonant *p* is silent, for example, when it is the second *p* in words like *supper* and *dipper*.
- ✓ It is also silent when followed by *n*, *s*, or *t* in words like *pneumonia, psychology,* and *pterodactyl.*
- ✓ When followed by the letter *h,* the combination makes an /f/ sound as in *phone,* and *phase.*

PRACTICE THIS

Patricia Peabody sipped pink lemonade at the fair.
She put her straw deep into the cup,
and patted her little puppy and ate a fat pear.
Then she sipped and sipped the lemonade all up.

Practicing the Consonant 

Background

- ✓ The letter *q* is unique since it almost always appears with the letter *u*.
- ✓ Sometimes the *u* following *q* is silent, as in the words *antique* and *bouquet*.

PRACTICE THIS

The quiet quail quoted to the quacking duck, saying quack, quack.

While the queen quite quickly questioned why the night was black.

The frequent quitter quickly picked up his equipment and quietly quit.

Practicing the Consonant 

Background

- ✓ Most often the /r/ sound in the initial, final, and medial positions is made by the consonant *r* as in the words *rat, ring, rocket, jar,* and *erase.*
- ✓ The use of the consonant *r* is very consistent for the /r/ sound.
- ✓ There are other letters and combinations of letters that also make the /r/ sound. The most common is *wr* in the words *write* and *wrist.*
- ✓ Other less common combinations include *rhy* in *rhyme, rps* in *corps* and *rt* in *mortgage.*
- ✓ Sometimes the consonant *r* is silent, as when it is doubled in words like *arrest.*

Practicing the Consonant 

Background

- ✓ Most often, the /s/ sound in the initial, final, and medial positions is made by the consonant *s* as in *set, sap, sand, bus,* and *beside.*
- ✓ The use of the consonant *s* is very consistent for the /s/ sound, although there are other letters and combinations of letters that also make the /s/ sound.
- ✓ These include *c* in the words *circus* and *circle,* and the *ps* combination as in *psychology.*
- ✓ Sometimes the consonant *s* is silent, for example, when it is doubled in words like *mess* and *dress.*

PRACTICE THIS

Sammy Snake sat under the Sun.

Practicing the Consonant 

Background

- ✓ Most often the /t/ sound in the initial, final, and medial positions is made by the consonant *t* as in *tap, pot,* and *little*.
- ✓ The use of the consonant *t* is consistent for the /t/ sound, although there are other letters and combinations of letters that also make the /t/ sound.
- ✓ Sometimes the consonant *t* is silent, for example, when it is the second *t* in words like *little* and *bottle,* and when it follows *s* and *f* in words like *listen* and *often*.
- ✓ It is also silent in many words of French origin such as *ballet* and *bouquet*.
- ✓ *T* appears in many digraphs, such as *th* and *tch,* and can represent the /ch/ and /sh/ sound in words like *motion* and *picture*.

PRACTICE THIS

Todd the toad sat in boat.
He wanted to row afar,
but the boat would not float.
So he sat and played a guitar.

Practicing the Consonant 

Background

- ✓ The letter *v* is a reliable letter in terms of the sound it makes.
- ✓ The letter *v* only makes the /v/ sound, as in the words *vice* and *van*.
- ✓ The /v/ sound also appears in the final position in words such as *five*, and in the middle position in words such as *never* and *even*.

PRACTICE THIS

Vinnie put a vine in a vase for Val as a valentine and then he took Val to a very fine place in the valley to dine.

Never ever put a violin in a van and drive over the river after five.

Practicing the Consonant 

Background

- ✓ The consonant *w* is a difficult consonant to learn since it is not all that reliable as a sound.
- ✓ Most often, it makes the /w/ sound at the beginning of a word or syllable, as represented in words such as *wit*, *wagon*, and *away*.
- ✓ When combined with vowels it takes on a different sound, such as with the diphthong *ow* in *now*.
- ✓ It can be a silent letter in words like *write* and *two*.

PRACTICE THIS

Wee Willy Winkle wore a wind-up watch as big as a wall.
His wife wore a weird wool wig that was as small as Wee Willy was tall.
We all couldn't wait until Willy walked with his wife through the mall.
Wally the worm wiggled backward along the sidewalk until he was halfway home.

Practicing the Consonant 

Background

- ✓ The letter *x* is not a frequently used letter, nor is it a reliable letter since the sounds assigned to it vary greatly.
- ✓ The most common sound representation is the /ks/ sound it makes when at the end of words such as *fox* and *mix*.
- ✓ *X* makes a /gz/ sound when it appears in the medial position, as it does in words such as *exit, exam,* and *exact*.
- ✓ Sometimes it makes the /z/ sound, as it does in words like *xylophone* and *xerox*.
- ✓ Occasionally *x* makes the /z/ sound when in the medial position as in *anxiety*. *X* even makes the sound of its own name in words such as *x-ray*, and is silent at the end of *Sioux*.
- ✓ There are other sounds assigned to *x*: /kzh/ in *luxury*, and /ksh/ in *anxious*.

PRACTICE THIS

The sounds of X

KS	**KZ**
Except	Exist
Extensive	Exactly
Extremely	Exams

Practicing the Consonant 

Background

- ✓ The letter *y* is used as a consonant less than 5% of the time.
- ✓ When it is a consonant, it usually appears at the front of a word or syllable as it does in *yellow, yam,* and *beyond.*
- ✓ A vast majority of the times *y* appears in a word, it is a vowel.
- ✓ When it is a vowel, it can be a long *i* as in *fly*, a long *e* as in *lady*, a short *i* as in *nymph,* and a long *a* when combined with the letter *a* as in *ray*.

PRACTICE THIS

The yellow yak said yes I like yeast and yolks.

But when I yodel and yawn you think its a joke.

The young goat wandered beyond yonder canyon and into Ying's backyard.

Practicing the Consonant 

Background

- ✓ The letter *z* is not a frequently used letter.
- ✓ The most common sound representation is the /z/ sound it makes in words like *zebra* and *zero*.
- ✓ The letter also makes the /z/ sound when in the medial and final positions, as in *fizz* and *frozen*.
- ✓ One *z* is silent when doubled in words such as *buzz* and *fuzz*.
- ✓ Actually, the letter *s* in words such as *is, was, rags, does*, and *rose* is more frequently used for the /z/ sound than the letter *z* itself.
- ✓ Among other letters used to make the /z/ sound are: *ss* as in *scissors*, *cz* as in *czar*, and *x* as in *xylophone*.

PRACTICE THIS

The six zebras zinged and zoomed as they zig-zagged through the center of town.

They were zapped by the zookeeper and zero zebras zoomed through town by sundown.

A buzzard the size of a zebra sipped zesty tea and snoozed to keep from freezing in the blizzard.

PRACTICE EXERCISES FOR CONSONANTS

A Story for B

One morning Brandon woke up to a loud B-B-B-B sound. He walked over to the window and looked down. He saw his big brother, Bobby, sitting on a brand new bike (motorbike). Bobby had a broad smile on his face as he checked and listened to the B-B-B-B of the engine. Brandon opened the window, held onto the frame, and shouted down, "Can I have a ride?" Bobby looked up and nodded his head slowly. Brandon quickly dressed and ran downstairs. He grabbed his black helmet before going out the back door. Bobby was sitting up proudly on his new bike, giving it gas and listening to the lip popping B-B-B-B of the engine. Brandon climbed on back and held tightly to his big brother's waist. He was glad he had a big brother and hoped that one day he could have a new bike too.

List of /b/ words:

boots	birthday	baseball	builder	barn
backpack	bill	bear	butter	bookcase
ball	baker	belt	bowl	bank
babysitter	bucket	bird	bell	box
bracelet	balloon	blocks	baby	blue

A Story for R

Randy loved cars. He especially loved racing cars and wanted to be a racecar driver when he grew up. He had a large box with a steering wheel and when he sat in it, he felt just like it was real. He would pretend to put a key in the ignition and he would turn it to start the engine. Sometimes, he forgot to put gas in it, and then the engine would have an R-R-R sound, but would not start. Then he would remember about the gas and would push his car over to a gas pump and fill the tank up to the rim. Once he got back in to start it, he would not hear the

R-R-R. He would hear a low, loud, RRROOM. Randy enjoyed racing his car on rainy days and today, it was pouring.

List of /r/ words:

rabbit	rainbow	radio	ring	race
rocket	rooster	rain	rain	rake
rattle	raisins	raccoons	red	rock
ribbon	rectangle	round	rice	rose
recipe	room	row	ruler	robot

Sylvia's Bike (A story for S)

Sylvia rushed home from school. It was her birthday and the only thing she had asked for was a shiny silver bike. She was absolutely sure she would get it. Her old bike was dull and had a slow leak in the back tire. If you put your ear close, you could hear the air escaping, (sssssss). When Sylvia arrived home, her grandfather was there to greet her. "Is my birthday present here yet?" she asked eagerly. "No, just be patient." Said her grandfather. Sylvia thought she had better take one final ride on her old decaying bike. She went to the shed and pulled out her bike, along with the tire pump. As she pumped up the back tire, she leaned close and heard the sssss of the air leaking out. She jumped quickly and rode to the corner and back before the tire became too flat to ride. Sylvia went inside and found her grandfather making soup and sandwiches for dinner. Her grandfather stopped to open the door for Sylvia's mom. Sylvia's mom walked in with a box wrapped for her birthday. Sylvia was immediately disappointed. She knew from the size that she did not get the new silver bike. The box was much too small to hold a new bike. Sylvia's mother handed her the box gave her a hug with a "Happy Birthday" wish. Sylvia slowly opened the box and found a can of silver spray paint and a new back tire. "Let me change my clothes and we'll go get to work." said Sylvia's mother. A simple, sincere, smile formed on Sylvia's face.

List of /s/ words:

soccer	submarine	saw	soup	six
soft	school	sun	summer	silver
seven	seal	star	simple	saddle
snow	snake	sailboat	smell	swim
sandwich	song	size	seeds	sit

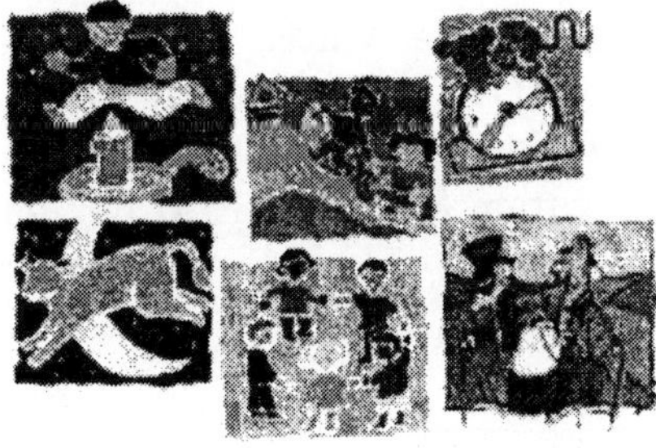

A Ticker (A story for T)

Taylor was walking down the sidewalk near her house when she saw the shiny object. She went closer to get a better look. As she got closer, she saw that it was a watch. She put it up to her ear and could hear the T-T-T-T tick and knew that it was working. Taylor put the watch in her pocket and took it home. She was tired and forgot about it until the next day. Taylor found the watch in the pocket of her jeans where she had left it the day before. She pulled the watch out and listened for the tick T-T-T-T. "Yes", she thought, it was still working.

She found her dad in the backyard and asked him about keeping the watch. Her father said, "It belongs to someone. We need to try to find the owner." "Come on in the house and I'll help you make a sign." Said her dad. Taylor followed her dad into the house and set the watch on the table. Her dad picked it up and put it to his ear and heard the T-T-T-T. "Yes, it seems to be working fine." He said. Taylor and her dad made ten signs about the watch. The owner could claim the watch if they could describe it. Taylor and her dad went around the neighborhood and taped up the signs. Then waited for a response. A week had passed without any word, but on Saturday morning, a telephone call came. The caller spoke in a timid voice and was able to describe the watch. Taylor was disappointed. She had secretly hoped that no one would call about the watch and she would get to keep it. An hour later, an elderly woman knocked on the door. Taylor went with her father to return the watch. The woman was excited about getting her watch returned. It had been a special present from her mother, but was stolen during a robbery. After the explanation, Taylor was happy that she had found the owner of the watch. She held it to her ear one last time and heard the T-T-T-T.

List of /t/ words:

tie	turtle	tiger	tire	teeth
turkey	telephone	toothbrush	tent	tape
tree	toe	tub	table	tea
top	tongue	toast	toad	tag
train	touch	teacher	tomorrow	ten

Vowel Sounds

Vowel Sounds can be divided into Long Vowel and Short vowel sounds:

Long Vowels:

These vowel sounds are longer in duration and can be stretched still further.

Short Vowels:

These vowels sound short or clipped. To make these vowels longer, or "stretched" we have to make slight adjustments to the positions of our tongue and jaw.

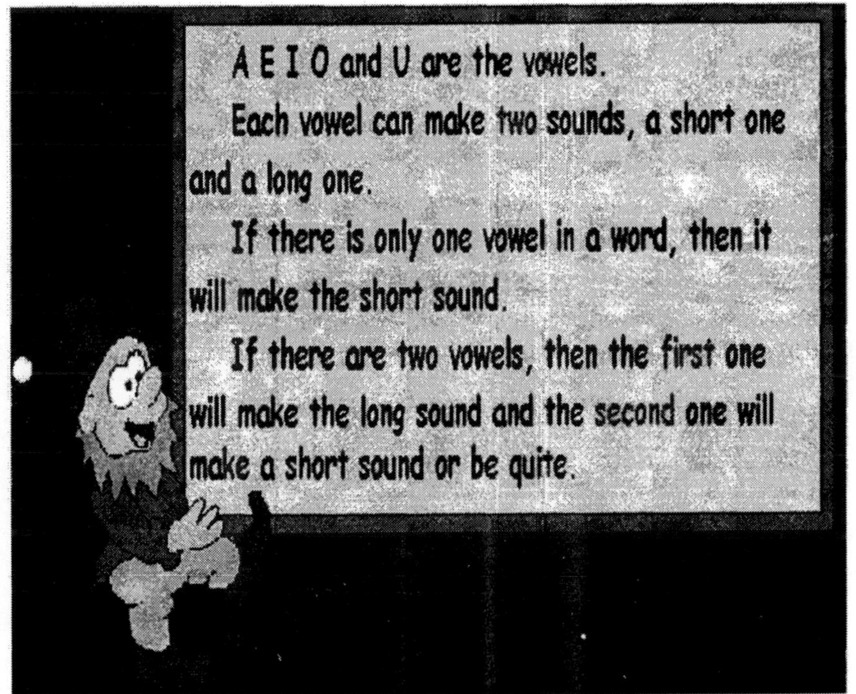

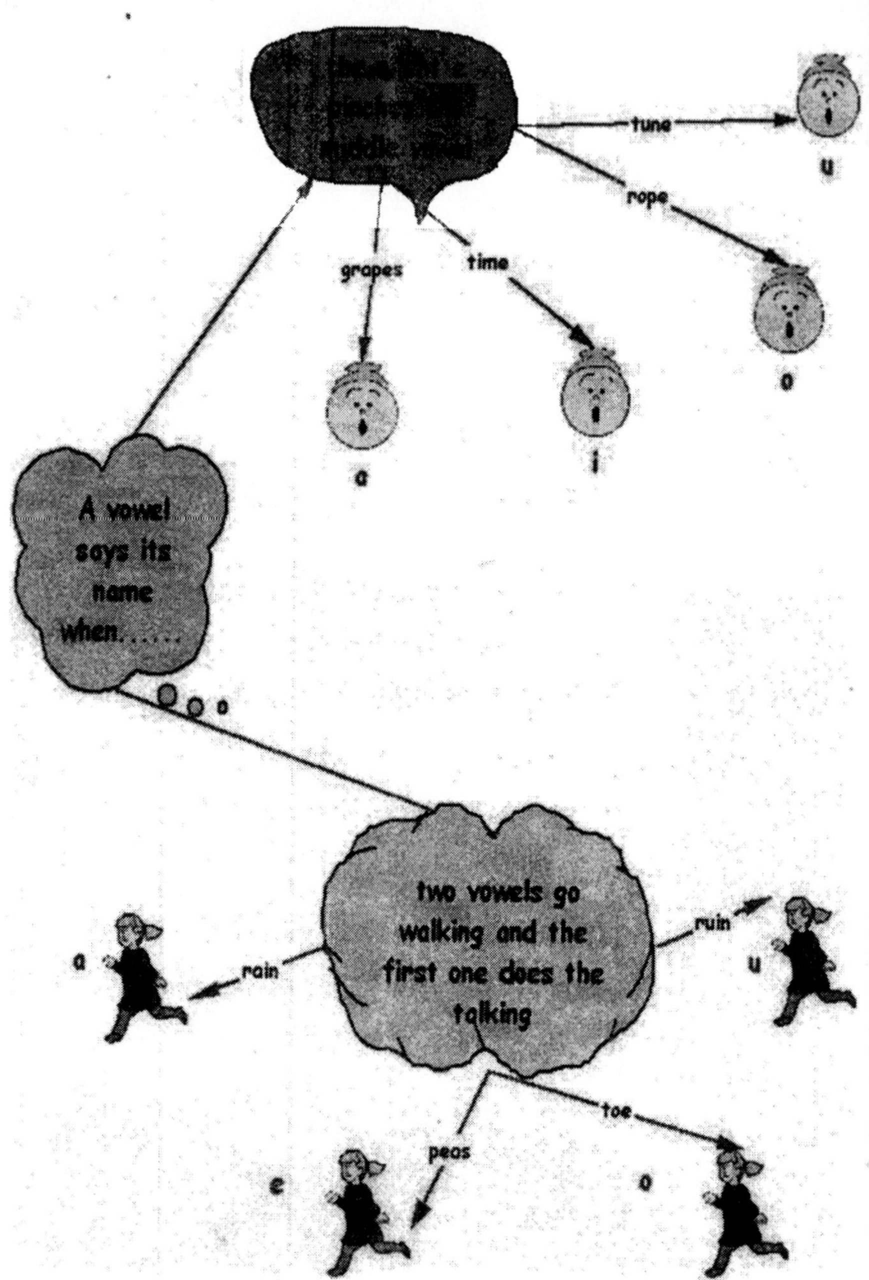
tune
u
rope
o
grapes
time
a
i
A vowel says its name when.......
two vowels go walking and the first one does the talking
a
rain
ruin
u
peas
toe
e
o

LONG VOWEL SOUNDS

Say the words out aloud. Remember to stretch the sound.

ü EE-'ieeeee' (Rhyme with He)

ü OO-'oooo' (Rhyme with Too)

ü AH-'aaaaa' (Rhyme with La)

ü Aww-'Awwww' (Rhyme with Saw)

ü ER-'errrrr' (Rhyme with Her)

EE	OO	AH	AWW	ER
Beet	Boot	Bath	Born	Burp
Cheek	Cooed	Cart	Corn	Curd
Deal	Drool	Dart	Dawn	Dirt
Feel	Fool	Far	Borrow	Burn
Greet	Who	Grass	Glory	Girl
Heat	Juice	Heart	Horse	Hirsute
Jeans	Cool	Jar	Jaunt	Germ
Key	Moose	Calm	Call	Worm
Meek	Pool	Mass	Morning	Lurk
Neil	Tool	Nazi	Lawn	Mirth
Peel	Stool	Pass	Pour	Pearl

SHORT VOWEL SOUNDS

Say the words out aloud. Remember to use short sounds.

Example: B-eh-t

✓ Eh-'ehh'

✓ i-'ih'

- ✓ oo-'oh'
- ✓ uh-'uhh'
- ✓ aw-'oaw'

Eh	**I**	**Oo**	**Uh**	**Aw**
Bet	Bit	Book	But	Bought
Check	Chick	Cook	Cut	Caught
Desk	Did	Push	Does	Dot
Debt	Fit	Foot	Fun	Frock
Fence	Grit	Good	Gut	Got
Get	Kill	Took	Cud	Cot
Ked	Lit	Look	Lump	Lottery
Let	Milk	Should	Muck	Mock
Men	Knit	Nook	Knuckle	Knock
Pet	Pit	Put	Putt	Popcorn
Said	Pick	Pull	Shut	Proper

PHONETIC SYMBOLS

These are symbols, which help a person know how to pronounce a word, which is unknown to them.

Survey of English phonetic symbols

Short vowels

1	[ɪ]	e.g. big, Britain, busy
2	[e]	e.g. desk, friend, weather
3	[æ]	e.g. cat, language, exactly
4	[ɒ]	e.g. hot, across, continent
5	[ʊ]	e.g. book, woman, full
6	[ʌ]	e.g. cut, butter, colourful
7	[ə]	e.g. afraid, London, breakfast

Long vowels

1	[iː]	e.g. tree, people, police
2	[ɑː]	e.g. basket, ask, photograph
3	[ɔː]	e.g. ball, blackboard, daughter
4	[uː]	e.g. blue, school, afternoon
5	[ɜː]	e.g. burn, girl, prefer

Commonly Mispronounced Words

Representative	rep-rhey-zent-titive
Regime	rhe-zhime
Schedule	skhey-jule
Sentence	sen-tense
Psychology	sai-kaww-lagy
Photography	futo-grufy
Biology	bye-aww-lagy
Forget	fuget
Pronunciation	pruh-nun-see-eh-shan
Probably	praww-bub-lee
Partial	pahr-shial
Precious	preh-shious
Police	poo-leace
Project (n)*	praww-ject
Pizza	peedza
Engage	en-gage
Enjoy	in-joy
Government	gah-vament
Monotony	mun-aww-tuny
Leisure	leh-zhure
Mortgage	maww-gage
Address (n)*	add-ress
Colony	caww-luny
Balcony	bahl-cuny
American	a-merry-kan

* (n)- stands for noun

Sounds of Speech

When you listen to speech you hear an almost continuous chain of sounds. You do not actually hear the boundaries of words. If you were asked to listen to Chinese and write down the separate words you would probably not be able to do that. In your head you are able to break down this chain into separate words because you are familiar with the sounds and can create meaningful words with them.

Creating sounds

You can view the lungs, throat, mouth and nose as a system of tubes and valves, which can regulate airflow. When you speak you actually breath out and direct the air through your throat and mouth or nose creating different sound. The sound largely depends on:

- ➲ Tongue
- ✓ Lips
- ✓ Vocal Cords

Tongue

Lifting the back or the front of the tongue makes some consonants:

Back: k,g

Front: t, d, th, l

Lips

The lips are used to make the *p* and the *b*.

The vocal cords

For vowels: the shape of the mouth (mainly determined by the position of the tongue). For consonants: the obstruction of airflow (by valves, tongue or lips)

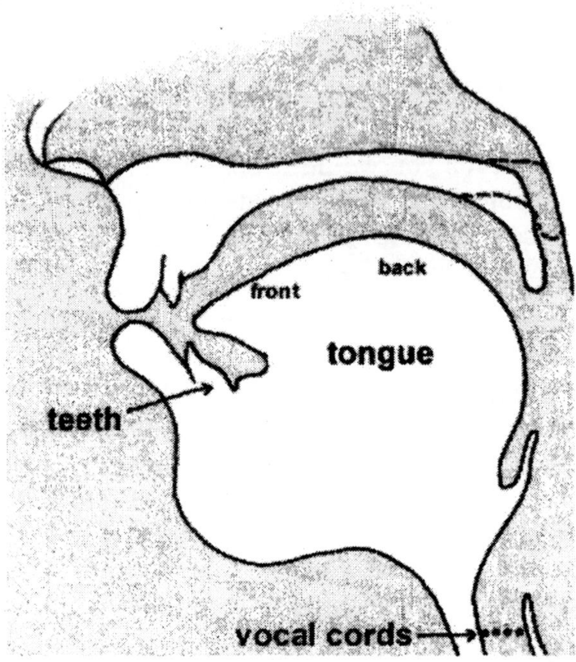

The vocal cords are used to make a sound voiced or voiceless.

Vowels are always voiced, but consonants can be voiced or voiceless.

For example, the difference between underlined sound in *prize* (voiced) and *price* (voiceless). Most consonants have a voiced and a voiceless version:

Voiced	**Voiceless**	**Compare**
b	p	be – pea
d	t	dear — tear
g	k	goat – coat (the *c* is also a *k* sound here)
z	s	zeal — seal
v	f	veal — feel

Vowels: the shape of the mouth

The shape of the inside of the mouth is mainly determined by the position of the tongue. The tongue can move up and down and from front to back.

By moving the tongue to a low position, the cavity in your mouth becomes larger and the sound sounds more like *a*-sound in *harm* or the *a* sound in *had*..

By moving your tongue up, the cavity becomes smaller and the sound is more like *i*-sound in *heed* or the *u* sound in *who'd*.

The shape of the lips also influences the sound.

Have a look at the lips and tongue positions when pronouncing different words.

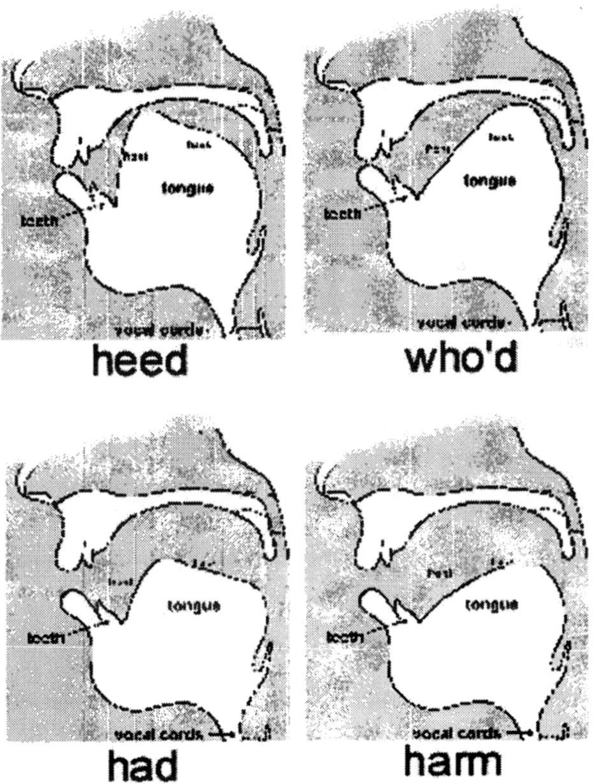

Stress

If you would record separate sounds and then paste them one after the other, it would be very difficult to understand the words and sentences. The reason is that not only the sounds are important, but also stress (=emphasis).

For example, there is a clear difference in meaning between *present* (=gift) and *present* (=to show).

Many dictionaries indicate not only the pronunciation of a word, but also the stress pattern.

It is mostly indicated by underlining the stressed part of the word (e.g. /likwid/ for liquid) or by putting an apostrophe-like symbol before the stressed part (/ |likwid/)

Long words often have one rather heavily stressed part (primary stress, often indicated with an apostrophe at the top of the line) and a part that is also stressed, but with less intensity (secondary stress, often indicated with an apostrophe at the bottom of the line).

Assignment

Find out how the following pairs are stressed.

Noun	Verb
(the) contract	(to) contract
(the) desert	(to) desert
(the) export	(to) export
(the) import	(to) import
(the) insult	(to) insult
(the) object	(to) object
(the) permit	(to) permit
(the) protest	(to) protest
(the) record	(to) record

SECTION 2—GRAMMAR BUILDER

1. You and grammar

Think about your previous language learning experiences. Has learning or understanding the grammar helped you? Do you enjoy grammar or find it very boring? Is it important to you to be perfectly accurate in everything you say and write, or are you happy if you are able to communicate your message, however ungrammatically? All language learners have their own different view as to how important it is for them to learn "grammar". For some learners it is very important to study the rules and patterns of grammar and others prefer to "acquire" grammar rather than studying it. However, taking an interest in grammar will help you.

2. Collect examples

When you have studied a new grammar point in Grammar Builder, which is a new one to you, collect examples of the pattern for a week. Check that, you understand from your examples the rules of pattern and choice that are behind this grammar point.

3. Revise regularly

Check over any new grammar that you have practised in Grammar Builder regularly. Keep a regular time in your study week to revise new grammar ideas and to practise them again.

4. Keep a record

Keep a record of the new grammar and the new words, which you learn in Grammar Builder. This means keeping a written record of new patterns that you have studied and any new rules that can be used to explain the use and the pattern.

The Sentence

When we speak or write we use words. These are generally used in groups.

Example: John sat on a chair

A group of words like this, which make complete sense, is called a sentence.

KINDS OF SENTENCES

- ✓ Declarative
- ✓ Interrogative
- ✓ Imperative
- ✓ Exclamatory

A sentence that makes a statement or assertion is called a **Declarative sentence.**

Example: He was in the room.

A sentence that asks a question is called an **Interrogative sentence**.

Example: Where do you live?

A sentence that expresses a command is called an **imperative sentence.**

Example: Be Quiet.

A sentence that expresses a strong feeling is called an **exclamatory sentence.**

Example: How beautiful this girl is!

Subject and Predicate

A sentence always has two parts:

ü **Subject**

ü **Predicate**

When we make a sentence we do two things:

We talk about some person or thing.—**SUBJECT**

We say something about that person or thing. –**PREDICATE**

The subject of a sentence usually comes first because we should have a subject to talk about.

However, in imperative sentences we leave out the subject sometimes.

Nouns

Nouns are words, which tell us about places, animals and things.

These are called naming words also.

There are 5 types of nouns:

- ✓ Proper Nouns
- ✓ Common Nouns
- ✓ Collective Nouns
- ✓ Abstract Nouns
- ✓ Maternal Nouns

Proper Nouns—These are the names of places, animals and things.

Common Nouns—These are names, which are common to a group.

Eg: Boys, girls, tables and chairs.

Collective Nouns—This as the name suggests is a name for things grouped together.

Eg: army, bouquet and fleet.

Abstract Nouns—This is used to name emotions and feelings.

Eg: Laughter, sorrow.

Material Nouns—These are used to name materials. ***Eg***: coal, diamond, petrol, diesel, etc.

Pronouns

Pronoun is a word, which replaces a noun. The categories of pronouns are:

- ✓ Personal Pronouns
- ✓ Reflexive or Empathetic Pronouns
- ✓ Demonstrative Pronouns
- ✓ Indefinite Pronouns

Personal Pronouns—Used instead of names of people.

- ✓ *He*
- ✓ *She*
- ✓ *It*
- ✓ *You*
- ✓ *They*
- ✓ *I*
- ✓ *We*

Reflexive and Empathetic Pronouns

In these **–self** is added to

- ✓ My
- ✓ Them
- ✓ Your
- ✓ Him
- ✓ Her
- ✓ Our

They are called reflexive or empathetic pronouns.

Demonstrative Pronouns

These are used to point out the objects, which they refer to and are therefore called demonstrative pronoun.

- ✓ This
- ✓ That
- ✓ Those
- ✓ These

This/These-Refers to what is close to hand

That/Those-Refers to what is far away

Indefinite Pronouns

Pronouns, which refer to persons or things in a general way but do not refer to any person or thing in a general way but do not refer to any person or things are called indefinite pronouns.

- ✓ Anybody
- ✓ Somebody
- ✓ Few
- ✓ Many
- ✓ Any
- ✓ Other
- ✓ None

Articles

The words **a, an, the** are called articles.

A OR AN

A or AN are called indefinite articles because they usually leave an indefinite impression of the person or thing spoken of.

Eg:A doctor; that is any doctor.

Using A or AN

- ✓ We use A or An with singular nouns only.
  Eg: A girl, an orange.
- ✓ We use 'a' with singular nouns, which begin with consonant sounds.
- ✓ We use 'an' with singular nouns which begin with vowel sounds.
- ✓ We also use 'a' before adjectives with consonant sounds and 'an' before adjectives with vowel sounds.

Eg: An honest shopkeeper.
A wonderful artist.

Article-The

- ✓ When we speak of someone or something for the first time we use "a" or "an" but when we speak of the same person or thing for the second time we use "the".
- ✓ We use 'the' when it is clear to the listener or reader which person or thing we are referring to
  Eg: My car is at the workshop on Delhi road.
- ✓ We us 'the' when there is only one such thing.
  Eg: Sky, moon.

✓ We usually use 'the' before ordinal numbers.

(An ordinal number is a number like first, second, etc.)

Eg: Joseph won the third prize.

✓ We use 'the' before some proper nouns such as:

(a) Names of oceans, rivers and sea.

Eg:-the Atlantic ocean.

(b) Names of most buildings, landmarks, monuments and natural wonders.

Eg: The National Museum, the Taj Mahal.

(c) Names of places containing 'of 'and people's titles containing 'of'.

Eg: The state of Uttar Pradesh./The General Manager of HDFC.

Prepositions

A Preposition is a word placed before a noun or a pronoun to show in what relation the person or thing denoted by it stands in regard to something else.

'PREPOSITION-THAT IS PLACED BEFORE'

Kinds of Prepositions:

Simple-at, by, for, etc.

Compound-about, above, along.

Phrase-according to, in place of.

Relations Expressed by Prepositions

1. Place-*Eg*: He went around the world.
2. Time-*Eg*:- We left after his birth.

3. Manner-He fought <u>with</u> courage.
4. Reason-He did it <u>for</u> our good.
5. Measure-The bank charges <u>interest</u> at 6%.
6. Contrast-<u>After</u> every effort one may fail.
7. Inference-His skill comes <u>from</u> practice.

Usage of some prepositions

IN & AT

✓ **In** is used with names of countries and large towns.

Eg: He lives in India.

✓ Whereas **at** is more often used when speaking of small towns and villages.

Eg:He lies at Andheri in Mumbai

✓ We use **in** with the names of streets and **at** when we give the house number.

Eg:He lives in Church street.

He lives at 45 Church street.

✓ We also use **at** when we talk about group activities and shops/workplaces. Did you see Shobha at the party?

ON

It is used when we think of a place as a surface.

Eg: Put it <u>on</u> the table.

TILL & TO

Till is used for time and **to** is used for place.

Eg: He slept till 8 p.m.

He walked to the road.

With & By

With often denotes the instrument and **by** the agent.

Eg: He killed two birds with one stone.

In & within

In before a noun denoting a period of time means at the end of; **within** means before the end of.

Eg: I shall return in an hour.

I shall return within an hour.

Beside and besides

Beside means at the side of and besides means in addition to.

Eg: He sat beside me.

He had two chocolates **besides** the ones he already ate.

Since and from

They are both used to denote some point of time. **Since** is used when there is no date specified. **From** is used when date is specified.

Eg: I have eaten nothing since yesterday.
I started working from 1st Jan.

Prepositions with means of Transport

- ✓ We use **by+ noun** when we talk about means of transport.

  Eg: By bicycle, by car, by train.

- ✓ We do not use by when reference is to a specific bicycle.

  Eg: He went there on my bike.

- ✓ We use 'on' to mean a specific bicycle, bus, train, ship, or plane and 'in' to mean a specific car, taxi, lorry or ambulance.

✓ We say on foot not by foot.

WORDS FOLLOWED BY PREPOSITIONS

TO-

Adapt, adhere, allot, apologize, appoint, aspire, attend, attribute, belong, consent, contribute, lead, listen, object, prefer, pretend, refer, revert, stoop, succumb.

FROM-

Abstain, cease, derive, deviate, differ, emerge, escape, exclude, preserve.

WITH-

Associate, bear, clash, coincide, comply, cope, correspond, disagree, fill, intrigue, part, Quarrel, side, sympathize.

OF-

Beware, boast, complain, despair, die, disapprove, dispose, dream,

For-feel, hope, care, mourn, wish, and yearn

IN- delight, excel, fall, glory, increase, and indulge, involve.

ON- comment, decide, and depend.

PRACTICE EXERCISE

He quarreled ___me____a trifle.

He readily compiled____ my request.

He is married ____my cousin.

He is incapable ___doing good work.

There is no exception ___this rule.

I am obliged____you___your kindness.

We should rely____our own efforts.

He is good____maths.

He has a passion____arguing.

He is very different____his brother.

Answers: with, over, with, to, of, to, to, for, on, in, for, from

Verbs

They are doing words, which talk of actions.

All verbs are divided into three forms.

Base Form	**Simple Past**	**Past Participle**
awake	awoke	awoken
beat	beat	beaten
become	became	become
begin	began	begun
bend	bent	bent
bet	bet	bet
bind	bound	bound
bite	bit	bitten
bleed	bled	bled
blow	blew	blown
break	broke	broken
bring	brought	brought
build	built	built
burst	burst	burst
buy	bought	bought
catch	caught	caught
choose	chose	chosen
come	came	come
cost	cost	cost
cut	cut	cut
deal	dealt	dealt

draw	drew	drawn
drink	drank	drunk
drive	drove	driven
eat	ate	eaten
fall	fell	fallen
feed	fed	fed
feel	felt	felt
fight	fought	fought
find	found	found
fly	flew	flown
forget	forgot	forgotten
freeze	froze	frozen
get	got	got
give	gave	given
go	went	gone
grow	grew	grown
hear	heard	heard
hide	hid	hidden
hit	hit	hit
hold	held	held
hurt	hurt	hurt
keep	kept	kept
know	knew	known
lead	led	led
leave	left	left
lend	lent	lent

let	let	let
lose	lost	lost
make	made	made
mean	meant	meant
meet	met	met
pay	paid	paid
put	put	put
quit	quit	quit
read	read	read
ride	rode	ridden
ring	rang	rung
rise	rose	risen
run	ran	run
say	said	said
see	saw	seen
sell	sold	sold
shine	shone	shone
shoot	shot	shot
show	showed	shown
shrink	shrank	shrunk
shut	shut	shut
sing	sang	sung
sink	sank	sunk
sit	sat	sat

sleep	slept	slept
slide	slid	slid
speak	spoke	spoken
spend	spent	spent
spin	spun	spun
spread	spread	spread
stand	stood	stood
steal	stole	stolen
stick	stuck	stuck
strike	struck	struck
swear	swore	sworn
swim	swam	swum
swing	swung	swung
take	took	taken
teach	taught	taught
tell	told	told
think	thought	thought
throw	threw	thrown
wear	wore	worn
win	won	won
write	wrote	written

To be

How to make the verb to be:

Singular	*Plural*
I am **rich.**	**We** are **poor.**

You are **German.**
He is **a footballer.**
She is **a dentist.**
It is **a new shop.**

You are **here.**
They are **in America.**

Short forms - for speaking

Singular

I am - **I'm**
You are - **You'**re
He is - **He's**
She is - **She's**
It is - **It's**

Plural

We are - **We'**re
You are - **You'**re
They are - **They'**re

Negatives

Singular
I am not **rich.**
You are not **German.**
He is not **a footballer.**
She is not **a dentist.**
It is not **a new shop.**

Plural
We are not **poor.**
You are not **here.**
They are not **in America.**

Tenses

Tense—The tense of a verb shows the time of an action or an event.

Verb—An action word/Doing word,

Eg: singing, dance, walk, pick, and do.

Helping verbs

Help the verb in making more sense

✓ **IS**-Used for singular things

✓ **AM**-Used only with present continuous in verbs and with nouns

- ✓ **ARE**-Used for plural things
- ✓ **HAVE**-Used to create more force
- ✓ **HAS**-Used to create more force

I HAVE
WE HAVE
YOU HAVE
YOU HAVE
HE/SHE HAS
THEY HAVE
IT HAS
SHEELA HAS

Tenses are divided into three:

- ✓ Present
- ✓ Paste
- ✓ Future

PRESENT TENSE

A verb that refers to the present time is said to be in the present tense.

	SINGULAR	*PLURAL*
1ST PER	I LIKE	WE LIKE
2nd PER	YOU LIKE	YOU LIKE
3rd PER	HE/SHE LIKES	THEY LIKE

The present tense can be divided into four forms:

Simple Present - ***I like***

Here the action is mentioned simply without anything being said about the completeness.

Present Continuous- ***I am liking***

Here action is incomplete and continuous.

Present Perfect- **I *have liked***

Here action is mentioned as finished, complete or perfect.

Present Perfect Continuous- ***I have been liking***

Here the action is going on continuously and has not completed at this present moment.

EXAMPLE OF PRESENT TENSE-VERB-"SPEAK"

(Three Forms of Verb)

SPEAK	***SPOKE***	***SPOKEN***

I speak
I am speaking
I have spoken (3rd form)

I have been speaking

We speak
We are speaking
We have spoken (3rd form)
We have been speaking

PAST TENSE

The past tense is used to indicate an action in the past.

A verb that refers to the past time is said to be in the past tense.

The past tense is divided into four forms:

Simple Past

(a) Used to indicate an action completed in the past. It often occurs with adverbs or adverb phrases of the past time.

Eg:I Received the letter yesterday.
She left school last year.

(b) Sometimes used without an adverb of time.
Eg:I learnt English in Nagpur.

(c) The simple past is also used for past habits.
Eg: He studied many hours every day.

Past Continuous

(a) Used to indicate an action going-on at sometime in the past. The time of the action may or may not be specified.

Eg: 1. We were listening to the radio all evening.
2. It was getting darker and darker.

(b) This tense is also used with words like –always continually for persistent habits in the past.

Eg: He was always grumbling.

Past Perfect

(a) Used to indicate an action completed before a certain moment in the past.
Eg: I met him in Delhi in 1996. I had seen him last five years before.

(b) If two actions happened in the past, it may be necessary to show which happened before the other. The past perfect is mainly used in such a situation.
Eg: 1. I had done my exercise when Hari came to see me.
2. I had written the letter before he arrived.

Past Perfect Continuous

(a) Used for an action that began before a certain point in the past and continued up to that time.

Eg: 1. At that time he had been writing a novel for two months.
2. When Mr. Mukherjee came to the school in 1995, Mr.Anand had already been teaching there for five years.

Future Tense

A verb that refers to a future time is said to be in the future tense.

Simple Future Tense

(a) The simple future is used to talk about things which we cannot control. It expresses the future as a fact.
Eg: I shall be twenty next week.

(b) We use this tense to talk about what we think or believe will happen in the future.
Eg: I think Pakistan will win the match.

(c) We also use this tense when we decide to do something at the time of speaking.
Eg: It is raining. I will take an umbrella.

Future Continuous Tense

(a) We use this tense to talk about actions, which will be in progress at a time in the future.
Eg: I suppose it will be raining when we start.

(b) We also use this tense to talk about actions in the future which are already planned or which are expected to happen in the normal course of things.
Eg: I will be staying here till Sunday.

Future Perfect Tense

This tense is used to talk about actions that will be completed by a certain future time.

Eg: 1. I shall have written my exercise by then.
2. He will have left before you go to see him.

Future Perfect Continuous Tense

This tense is used for actions, which will be in progress over a period of time that will end in the future.

Eg: By next March we shall have been living there for four years.

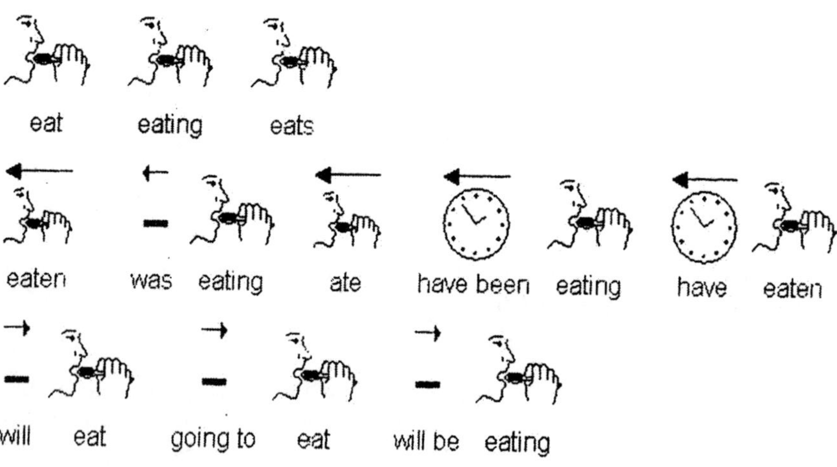

TENSES SYSTEM

VIEWS OF THE PRESENT

1. **He does**
2. **He is doing**
3. **He has done**
4. **He has been doing**

PAST TENSES

5. **He did**
6. **He was doing**
7. **He had done**
8. **He had been doing**

VIEWS OF THE FUTURE

1. He will do
10. He will be doing
11. He is going to do
12. He is doing
13. He is to do
14. He is about to do

VIEWS OF THE FUTURE

15. He will do
16. He would be doing
17. He would have done
18. He would have been doing

SECTION 3— VOCABULARY BUILDER

Improving your Vocabulary

When improving your vocabulary, it is important that you learn the word or expression in a practical way.

Through this section we have tried to make vocabulary as easy and practical to use.

The meanings have been given in the form of a sentence, which is easy to use.

1. Relationships with Other People

Our Lives

We have different stages in our life. Which stage are you in? Here are the main stages, which we go through:

Age	Name of the stage
0	newborn baby
0-2	baby
2-3	toddler
4-12	child
13-19	teenager
14-18	adolescent
20-29	in your twenties
30-39	in your thirties
40-60	middle-aged
60+	senior citizen

Relationships and Status

Here are the types of relationships people have and different ways of talking about people's status.

- ✓ If someone is **single,** they are not married.
- ✓ If someone is your **ex,** you did have a relationship with them but you do not anymore *e.g.* **ex-girlfriend.**
- ✓ If you have a **boyfriend / girlfriend,** you have a romance with them.
- ✓ If two people are **engaged,** they are going to get married soon.
- ✓ If someone is **married,** they have a husband or wife.
- ✓ If two people are **a couple,** they are together and may or may not be married.
- ✓ If you have **a partner,** you live with someone but are not married to him or her.
- ✓ We all have **best friends.**
- ✓ We also have our own **group of friends.**
- ✓ If married people split up, they first **get separated** and then they **get divorced.**
- ✓ If your husband or wife is dead, you are **widowed**. If you are the surviving man, you are a **widower**. If you are the surviving woman, you are a **widow**.

2. Feelings

We all have very many different feelings, which we experience. Here are some words, which describe those feelings:

- ✓ If you feel **upset,** you are not very happy.
- ✓ If you feel **confident,** you are sure that you can do something.
- ✓ If you feel **angry,** you hate something, which happened

to you.

✓ If you feel **worried**, you feel that something bad may happen.

✓ If you feel **bored**, you are not interested at all.

✓ If you feel **excited**, you feel happy waiting for an event to happen.

✓ If you are **interested in** something, you want to spend time doing it.

✓ If you feel **anxious**, you are a little afraid or worried about something.

✓ If you feel **embarrassed**, you think you look stupid.

✓ If you feel **nervous**, you are worried about something, which is going to happen to you.

✓ If you feel **afraid** or **frightened**, you fear something.

3. Character

We all have different characters. Here are some common adjectives used to describe people's characters.

✓ If someone **is optimistic**, they think the future will be good, but if someone is **pessimistic**, they think the future will be bad.

✓ If someone is **intelligent**, they are quick and clever at many things.

✓ If someone is **generous**, they give things to other people.

✓ If someone is **happy-go-lucky**, they do not worry about things.

✓ If someone is **boring**, they have nothing about them, which is interesting.

- ✓ If someone is **reckless** or **careless**, they are not very careful.
- ✓ If someone is **patient**, they will spend a lot of time doing something - the opposite is **impatient.**
- ✓ If someone is **big-headed**, they think they are very good at something (they might not be thought).
- ✓ The opposite of big-headed is **modest.**
- ✓ If someone is **selfish**, they only think about themselves - the opposite is **unselfish**.
- ✓ If someone is **brave**, they don't worry about danger.
- ✓ If someone is **two-faced**, they tell different people different things.
- ✓ If someone is **hard-working**, they work a lot.
- ✓ If someone is **ambitious**, they want to be successful.
- ✓ Someone who is **sensible**, does not do stupid things.
- ✓ If someone is **spiteful**, they say nasty things about other people.
- ✓ Someone who is **unusual**, does things in a different way.

4. Our Looks

What do you look like? What adjectives would you use to describe yourself? Here are some common adjectives used to describe what people look like.

- ✓ If you are very thin, we say you are **skinny**.
- ✓ Someone who is **overweight** is too fat.
- ✓ An **elegant** woman has expensive clothes.
- ✓ A **fashionable** person wears the latest clothes.
- ✓ People (men) who are strong and have lots of muscles are **well-built.**

- ✓ A **gorgeous** person, is very attractive.
- ✓ We can also say they are **stunning** - if they are attractive.
- ✓ You can describe someone by talking about their hair *e.g.*, has **long** / **short** hair, has **straight** / **curly** hair, has **fair** / **dark** hair.
- ✓ If someone looks **athletic**, they look as though they do lots of sports - the opposite is **unfit**.

5. Films

Do you like going to the movies? Here are some words we use about going to the movies:

- ✓ We can talk about **movies** or **films** - they mean the same thing.
- ✓ We go to watch movies **at the cinema**.
- ✓ You can **book** seats in advance.
- ✓ We say The Action Man is **on at the cinema**.
- ✓ Very popular movies may be **sold out** - so you can't get a seat.
- ✓ Movies are shown on a **screen**.
- ✓ The area inside a cinema is called the **foyer**. People meet each other in the **foyer**.
- ✓ People like to buy **popcorn** to eat during the movie.
- ✓ A very popular film is also called a **blockbuster**.
- ✓ The **box office** is the general term for money made by films.
- ✓ You can read **reviews** of new films to decide if you want to go and see them.

- ✓ When you are watching a film, you are part of the **audience**.
- ✓ If a film is not in your language, it will have **subtitles**. **Subtitles** are the words being spoken in the film, which are written in your language for you to read. They are at the bottom of the screen.
- ✓ Sometimes, if a film is not in your language, it is **dubbed**. This means the words are translated and spoken in your language.

The important parts of films

All of these things are important in making a film:

- ✓ To create a film, we say a film **is made**. Many films **are made** in Hollywood.
- ✓ The **star** of a film is the most important character in the story.
- ✓ The star has the **leading role** in the movie. When a person is **starring** in a film, they are the most important actor in this movie.
- ✓ There are also **co-stars** in movies.
- ✓ People who act in films are called **actors** and **actresses**.
- ✓ We say actors/actresses **play the role of** someone or **act** in a film.
- ✓ The **director** is the person who tells everyone what to do. He is in-charge of the film.
- ✓ All films start with a written **script**. The **script** has the story and the words in it.
- ✓ The **plot** of a movie is its story.
- ✓ The music, which is in a film, is called the **soundtrack**.
- ✓ All films have a **budget** - the amount of money, which it takes to make a film.
- ✓ Expensive films are called **big-budget** movies.
- ✓ The **special effects** in films are things like car crashes and explosions.

Types of Movies

There are many different types of films. Which do you prefer?

- ✓ A **comedy** is a film, which makes you laugh.
- ✓ A **romantic film** is about a love story.
- ✓ An **action movie** has lots of car chases and explosions in it.
- ✓ A **horror movie** will frighten you.
- ✓ **Cartoons** are made from drawings and often are for children.
- ✓ A **western** is a movie about cowboys and Indians.
- ✓ A **thriller** is a film with an exciting story usually about a crime.
- ✓ **War movies** are about wars - real (Second world war, Vietnam, etc) or imaginary futuristic ones.
- ✓ **Science fiction** movies are about the future or about travel in space.
- ✓ **Independent films** are made with a small budget and are about unusual topics.
- ✓ **Teen movies** are especially for teenagers.

Talking about films

What are your favourite types of films? Here are some adjectives and phrases, which you can use to describe films you have seen:

- ✓ Bad
- ✓ It was awful!
- ✓ I didn't enjoy it at all!
- ✓ Very slow and dull.
- ✓ Good
- ✓ It was fantastic, great fun.
- ✓ It was amazing; I am going to see it again.
- ✓ Brilliant, great acting.
- ✓ Comedies: really funny, hilarious.
- ✓ Romantic films: heart warming, it made me cry.

- ✓ Action movies: great special effects, very fast.
- ✓ Horror movies: very scary, it made me jump.
- ✓ Thrillers: exciting, a great plot.

6. Crime and Criminals

A crime is an action, which is against the law. There are many different types of crimes and here are some of the most common.

1. Violent crimes

These are all violent crimes, which usually involve people being hurt:

- ✓ A **murder** happens when someone kills another person.
- ✓ An **assault** happens when a person attacks and hurts another person.
- ✓ If there is a **stabbing**, someone is attacked with a knife.
- ✓ An **act of terrorism** happens when people use bombs and murder for political reasons.
- ✓ If a person is captured and held by other people, this is a **kidnap**. The kidnappers ask for money to return the captured person.
- ✓ To take someone's wallet in the street by attacking them is called **mugging**.
- ✓ When sex takes place against someone's will, this is called **rape**.
- ✓ If a building is set on fire deliberately, this is an act of **arson**.
- ✓ When a plane or a coach is taken over by people, it is a **hijack**.
- ✓ A **hit-and-run** happens when a car crashes into a person and then does not stop.

2. Crimes committed for money

These types of crime are committed for money or to gain things. They are all nouns.

✓ **Stealing** occurs when someone takes things which do not belong to him / her.

✓ The crime of **drug dealing** involves selling illegal drugs such as heroin.

✓ A **forgery** is produced when a criminal copies something of value such as a painting.

✓ **Blackmail** happens when a person asks for money and in return offers not to tell other people about inappropriate behaviour.

✓ When people have their wallets taken from their pockets or handbags, it is called **pick pocketing**.

✓ **Fraud** happens when people get money from others by illegal means, which involves deceiving them.

✓ **Shoplifting** is the act of stealing from a shop.

✓ If drugs or large quantities of alcohol or cigarettes are taken from one country to another illegally, this is **smuggling**.

✓ When a person goes into a house and takes things it is a **burglary**.

✓ Burglary is also called a **break-in.**

3. Minor crimes

These are types of crime which are considered minor:

✓ An act of **vandalism** occurs when public places are damaged.

✓ **Graffiti** is writing on places, which are public such as walls.

✓ **Dangerous driving** is driving without using the rules of the traffic.

- ✓ To drive after drinking alcohol is called **drunk driving**.
- ✓ If you are caught for **speeding**, you are driving faster than the speed limit.
- ✓ **Petty crime** is the name given to all the crimes, which are minor.
- ✓ **Football hooliganism** involves many problems connected to football fans.

The criminals

People who have committed crimes are called criminals. Here is a table of the crimes described above with the word for the person who commits each type of crime:

Type of crime	The criminal who commits the crime
murder	murderer
assault	assailant or attacker
act of terrorism	terrorist
kidnap	kidnapper
mugging	mugger
rape	rapist
arson	arsonist
hijack	hijacker
stealing	thief
drug dealing	drug dealer
forgery	forger
drunk driving	drunk driver
blackmail	blackmailer
pick pocketing	pick pocketer
fraud	fraudster
shoplifting	shoplifter

smuggling	smuggler
vandalism	vandal
burglary	burglar
petty crime	petty criminal
hooliganism	hooligan

7. Sounds and Noises

There are many different types of sounds, which we make with our voices. These are sounds, which do not have words with them. The sounds usually show how you feel about something.

- ✓ To **whistle** is to blow air through your teeth and lips so as to make a musical tune.
- ✓ A **wolf-whistle** is a special type of whistle, which men make at attractive women or vice-versa.
- ✓ You **hum** with your lips closed and make a sound with your throat. You can **hum** tunes.
- ✓ A **cough** is the noise you make when you clear your throat. Smokers cough a lot.
- ✓ You might make a **crunch** when you chew something hard.
- ✓ If you **sigh**, you make a noise when you breathe out to show you are tired or unhappy.
- ✓ A **groan** is a loud noise, which you make when you get bad news.
- ✓ To **snore** is to make a sound when you are asleep. You **snore** through your nose.
- ✓ You **sniff** with your nose to clear it.
- ✓ If you **slurp** a drink, you drink it noisily and fast.
- ✓ A **gulp** is a noise made by a loud swallow.
- ✓ You make a **tut**, if you disapprove of something.

- ✓ If you go **sshhh**, you show that you want someone else to stop speaking.
- ✓ A **gasp** is a sharp intake of air. You usually gasp when you are shocked by some sudden news.

1. Noises, which accompany actions

These words all describe actions, which also have a noise or a sound, which accompanies them:

- ✓ A **bang** is a general word for any short, loud noise.
- ✓ A doorbell or the telephone will **ring**.
- ✓ A **click** is the sound of a door closing quietly or of a computer mouse.
- ✓ When you **scratch**, you use your nails to touch your skin.
- ✓ There is a **bang** when a door closes very quickly.
- ✓ A clock **ticks**.
- ✓ If your clock makes a noise at every hour, this is a **chime**. Clocks **chime** the same number of times as the hour they are indicating.
- ✓ If a book falls on the floor, it makes a **thump**.
- ✓ An **explosion** is the action and the sound of a bomb going off.
- ✓ A **crash** is the action and sound of two cars hitting each other.
- ✓ When brakes are put on very hard, a car makes a **screech**.
- ✓ When you open a newspaper, it makes a **rustle**.
- ✓ A **splash** is the sound of something going into water.
- ✓ A burning fire will **crackle**.

2. Animal noises

Have you got any pets? Do you know what the words are in English for the sounds they make? Here are some of the words for the sounds, which different animals make:

- ✓ A sheep **baas.**
- ✓ If a cat **meows,** it makes a sound with its voice.
- ✓ When a cat is happy, it **purrs.**
- ✓ A dog **barks.**
- ✓ Hens **cluck.**
- ✓ Geese and snakes **hiss.**
- ✓ A lion or a tiger **roars.**
- ✓ A cow **moos**.
- ✓ A mouse **squeaks**.
- ✓ Most birds sing, but doves **coo**.
- ✓ A horse **neighs** and a donkey **brays**.
- ✓ Bees and wasps **buzz**.

3. Musical sounds

There are many different words, which describe types of musical sounds:

- ✓ The **tone** of a sound is its quality.
- ✓ A **note** is a sound used in music. The notes go from A to G.
- ✓ A **bass** sound is a deep musical sound, for example: made from the bass guitar.
- ✓ A **treble** sound is a high sound.
- ✓ A **high-pitched** sound is very squeaky.
- ✓ The **beat** of music is its stress or its louder notes.
- ✓ The **rhythm** of the music is the way it moves and the general pattern it has. So there is a rock and roll **rhythm** or a salsa **rhythm**.

8. Illness

Types of Illness

There are many different types of illnesses, which humans can get. Some illnesses are serious and we may die from them. Here are some of the most common illnesses:

- ✓ A **disease** is any illness caused by an infection or by bacteria.
- ✓ An **infection** is a disease, which you can catch from other people who have one.
- ✓ A **virus** is a germ, which causes illnesses such as flu.
- ✓ If you have an **allergy** to something, then when you come into contact with it or eat it your body has a bad reaction. Many people **are allergic to** nuts, for example.
- ✓ **Flu** is a common illness and results in people having a fever and aches.
- ✓ A **heart attack** occurs when the heart stops working correctly.
- ✓ There are many different types of **cancer**. **Cancer** is the growth of bad cells in a body and **lung cancer** is one of the most common **cancers**.
- ✓ A **tumour** is a large growth on an organ of the body such as the brain.
- ✓ If people **have a stroke**, their heart has a sudden problem.
- ✓ An **ulcer** is a painful area of skin, which is often yellow or white in colour. We often get ulcers in our mouth and in our stomach.
- ✓ **Appendicitis** is a severe pain in the appendix. You usually have to have the appendix removed by an operation.
- ✓ **Chickenpox** usually happens to young children. The symptoms are red spots and a fever.

- ✓ **Asthma** is a disease, which causes great difficulty in breathing.
- ✓ **Mental illness** is the general term for many different kinds of problems with the mind and the brain.
- ✓ **Depression** is a common type of mental illness. It causes people to have very negative ideas and thoughts about life.
- ✓ When a person is **paralysed**, he or she cannot move all or parts of their body.
- ✓ **Arthritis** is a disease of the joints in the body, which makes it difficult to move parts of the body.
- ✓ A **migraine** is a very severe headache.
- ✓ If we eat old or bad food, we can get **food poisoning**.
- ✓ A **coma** is a state where people are unconscious for a long time.

People and places connected to illness

Here are the words for some of the people and the places, which are connected to illnesses:

- ✓ The first person you tell about an illness is usually your **doctor**. A **doctor** is also called a **GP (general practitioner)**.
- ✓ The **patient** is a person who is being treated for an illness.
- ✓ A **nurse** is a person who helps doctors look after ill people.
- ✓ A **consultant** is a very experienced and skilled doctor who knows a lot about one specific kind of illness. **Consultants** are also called **specialists**.
- ✓ A **surgeon** is a doctor with special skills in operations.
- ✓ The **anaesthetist** is a person in a hospital who makes people unconscious before operations.
- ✓ A **paramedic** is a person with some medical training who helps with ill people.
- ✓ A **physiotherapist** helps people with problems of body movement.

- ✓ A **ward** is a section of a hospital with beds for ill people.
- ✓ An **operation theatre** is the place where operations take place.
- ✓ The **accident and emergency unit** is a place in the hospital where ambulances bring newly ill people such as those who have had car crashes.

Actions, which are connected to illness

Here are some of the common verbs, which are used to talk about illnesses:

- ✓ When a doctor **diagnoses** your illness, he or she tells you what illness you have.
- ✓ When an illness has gone, the patient is **cured**.
- ✓ When an illness is going, a patient is **recovering** or **getting better**.
- ✓ If you are **taken ill**, an illness has begun.
- ✓ If a patient **deteriorates**, he or she gets worse and the illness becomes more serious.
- ✓ In an emergency, people are **rushed** to **hospital**.
- ✓ A surgeon **operates** on ill people.
- ✓ An anaesthetist **puts people to sleep** before an operation.
- ✓ When a part of our body is replaced it is called a **transplant**.
- ✓ We **have an injection** to prevent us getting some illnesses.
- ✓ We say that we **catch a cold** or **catch the flu.**
- ✓ At a doctor's you need to **describe your symptoms**.
- ✓ A doctor can **prescribe** tablets or medicine, which you need to buy from a pharmacy or a chemist's.
- ✓ When you are ill, you will **need a course of treatment**.
- ✓ When we say a person **suffers** from an illness, they are feeling bad because of it.
- ✓ Infectious diseases **spread** from person to person.

9. Senses

There are five senses, which humans have. These are smell, hearing, seeing, taste and touch. Here are the common words and some idiomatic uses connected to our senses.

Smell

The sense of smell comes through our nose. Here are some common words associated with smell:

- ✓ Of is always used with smell to describe types of smells. For example, Her room smelled of roses or It **smells of** cigarettes.
- ✓ Our **nostrils** are the two passages in our nose, which take air into our bodies.
- ✓ The top of the nose is called the bridge of the nose.
- ✓ To **sniff** is to quickly breathe in through the nose.
- ✓ When we want to talk about a very powerful smell, we usually say a **strong smell**.
- ✓ An **aroma** is a very pleasant smell, often a smell of food which is cooking.
- ✓ If there is a smell, which you do not recognise or do not like, it is called a **funny smell**.
- ✓ An **odour** is a bad smell.
- ✓ When we want to get rid of bad smells we use an **air-freshener**. This often comes in an aerosol can and we spray it in the room.

Hearing

The sense of hearing comes through our ears. Here are some of the common words associated with the sense of hearing:

- ✓ The general word for things we hear is a **sound**.
- ✓ Sounds can be **loud** or **quiet.**

- ✓ When we talk very quietly so that no-one can hear, we **whisper**.
- ✓ People who cannot hear are **deaf**.
- ✓ When a person has difficulty hearing, they are described as **hard of hearing**.
- ✓ A person who is hard of hearing might use a **hearing aid** to help them.
- ✓ Deaf people communicate using **sign language**. **Sign language** is carried out with the hands.
- ✓ Deaf people may also **lip-read** to understand what people are saying.
- ✓ If a sound can be heard, it is **audible**.

Seeing

The sense of seeing comes through our eyes. Here are some of the common words associated with the sense of seeing:

- ✓ **Sight** is the noun from seeing.
- ✓ A person who is **shortsighted** cannot see long distances. Also a person who is **long-sighted** cannot see or read things, which are close to them.
- ✓ People who have difficulty seeing will either wear **glasses** or wear **contact lenses**. **Contact lenses** go into your eyes.
- ✓ A person who cannot see at all is **blind**.
- ✓ We say a person who can see is **sighted**.
- ✓ Blind people may have a **guide dog** to help them walk on the street.
- ✓ If books are written in **braille**, blind people can feel the words and are able to read them.
- ✓ Some people have difficulty distinguishing colours such as red and green. We say they are **colour blind**.
- ✓ **Reading glasses** are used to help long-sighted people read newspapers etc.

- ✓ People, who have a **squint**, have eyes, which look in different directions.
- ✓ A person, who is **cross-eyed**, has eyes, which look towards each other.
- ✓ The **pupil** is the centre part of an eye.
- ✓ The **eyelid** is the outer part of the eye, which opens and closes.
- ✓ An **eyelash** is a small hair on an eyelid.
- ✓ If you **have an eye for** something, you are good at it. For example, He has a good eye for a ball.
- ✓ If you **keep an eye on something**, you look after a person's possessions while they are away.

Touch

The sense of touch comes through our fingers. Here are some of the common words associated with the sense of touch:

- ✓ We use our **fingertips** to touch things.
- ✓ When we touch something for a specific purpose, we also **feel** it.
- ✓ Things can feel **smooth**, which means they are flat.
- ✓ Things can also feel **rough**, which means they have a surface which is not flat.
- ✓ We can say a place or an action **needs a woman's / man's touch**, which means it needs a woman / man to organise it.
- ✓ If we **keep in touch** with people like our friends, we do not lose contact with them.
- ✓ In speech, if a person **touches on** something, they talk about it briefly.

Taste

The sense of taste comes through our mouth and tongue. Here are some of the common words associated with the sense of taste:

- ✓ **Taste** is also a verb which means to eat a little of something to decide if you like it or not.
- ✓ There are five main **flavours**, **which** we can taste in food, sweet, sour, bitter, salty and spicy.
- ✓ A **sweet** flavour means that it tastes like sugar.
- ✓ A **bitter** taste means it tastes like it needs sugar in it.
- ✓ A **sour** taste means it tastes sharp like a lemon.
- ✓ A **salty** taste means it tastes like it has salt in it.
- ✓ If you think that a certain meal is **tasty**, it means you like it a lot.
- ✓ If something tastes **off,** it tastes like it is bad or unhealthy to eat.
- ✓ A **spicy** taste means the food tastes as if it has a lot of herbs and spices in it.
- ✓ If food like curry tastes **hot**, it burns your mouth a little bit.
- ✓ If you **get a taste for** something, you wish to do it again and again.

10. Meals and Cooking Food

Types of Meals

There are many ways in which we can eat and many types of meals which we eat. Which is your favourite way of eating? Here are the words for some of the different kinds of meals we eat:

- ✓ A take-away meal is one you buy and take to your home to eat. **Chinese meals** are a popular take-away in the UK.
- ✓ **Frozen meals** are ready prepared and can be bought from the supermarket.
- ✓ **Meals for one** can also be bought from the supermarket.
- ✓ Foods such as burgers are also called **junk food**. This is also called **fast food**.
- ✓ Many people like **eating out**, which is the phrase used for eating in restaurants.

✓ **Cordon bleu** cooking is very refined cooking done by an expert.

✓ A **picnic** is a meal, usually of sandwiches, eaten outside.

✓ A **barbecue** is a meal, usually of meat, cooked outside over hot coals.

✓ A **snack** is a small and quick meal.

✓ **TV dinners** are a type of frozen meal which you can buy from a supermarket. They have all the parts of a meal, vegetables, meat, etc. included.

✓ **Home cooking** is the type of food your mother prepares.

✓ **Vegetarian** meals are those without meat.

✓ Many people now like to eat **organic** food. Organic food has been produced without any chemicals.

✓ **Vegan** meals are those without any animal products like milk in them.

✓ **Brunch** is a large breakfast eaten near lunch time.

Ways of cooking food

Do you like cooking? Here are some verbs which describe the actions which are involved in different types of cooking:

✓ When you **roast** meat, it is cooked in the oven for some hours.

✓ We **boil** vegetables like potatoes.

✓ To **grill** food is to cook it by heating it from above.

✓ We deep fry foods such as chips.

✓ A **flambé** steak is cooked and set on fire briefly just before you eat it.

✓ Many people now **microwave** their food.

✓ We often cook food such as fish or rice by **steaming** it.

✓ When food **simmers**, it is kept boiling slowly.

✓ Foods such as stews are cooked in a **slow cooker.**

- ✓ People use **woks** to cook Chinese food.
- ✓ To cook bread you need to **bake** it in an oven.
- ✓ You need to **set the timer** to know how long your food has been cooking.

Preparing food before and while cooking it

Here are some of the verbs used to describe different ways of preparing food before you cook and for things you might do while cooking it.

- ✓ When you are preparing the ingredients before you start using them, you need to **weigh** or **measure** them to check you have the correct quantity.
- ✓ If you get meat out of your freezer, you need to **defrost** it or **thaw** it before you can cook it.
- ✓ If you **whisk** foods such as eggs, you stir them very quickly in order to get air into the mixture.
- ✓ While cooking food you may need to **stir** it with a spoon.
- ✓ To put liquid such as a sauce on food, is to pour it.
- ✓ After cooking vegetables in water, you **strain** them or **drain off** the water.
- ✓ We **slice** or **chop up** vegetables such as carrots before cooking them.
- ✓ We **peel** vegetables such as potatoes before cooking them.
- ✓ To get small strands of cheese, we **grate** it.
- ✓ When cooking with eggs, you first need to **break** or **crack** them.
- ✓ If you **grease** a dish or a pan, you put oil or butter on it before you start to cook with it.
- ✓ With some types of meals, you need to **stuff** meat or vegetables. This means put other ingredients inside.

Preparing food before eating it

Here are some of the verbs used to describe different ways of preparing food before you eat it:

- ✓ Before you eat a salad, you might **add** salad dressing.
- ✓ When we squash food such as potatoes, it is called to **mash** them.
- ✓ If you put food on top of a meal to make it look pretty, you **garnish** it.
- ✓ If you **season** food, you add spices or salt and pepper to alter the taste.
- ✓ If you **spread** something like butter onto bread, you put it on evenly.
- ✓ If roast meat has been cooked, you need to **carve** it into different portions.
- ✓ If there is any food left, you can **freeze** it to use again.

10. Collocations about People

Collocations are pairs (or more) of words which occur together. In speech or written English a very large combination of words are possible. However, some combinations are much more likely to be used than others. For example, we always say stale bread not bad bread or old bread and fish and chips not chips and fish. Here are some of the important collocations arranged around words connected to people. The words in the collocation are written in blue.

Baby

- ✓ When a woman is pregnant, she is **expecting a baby**.
- ✓ Couples who have no children of their own, sometimes decide to **adopt a baby**. Many adopted babies come from orphan houses.
- ✓ Babies can stop us sleeping and **keep us up all night**.

- ✓ If babies are born early, they are **premature babies.**

Child

- ✓ A woman will **give birth to a child.**
- ✓ Parents **bring up their children**.
- ✓ Sometimes when parents give their children too many things, they **spoil children.**
- ✓ Children born outside of marriage are called **illegitimate children.**

Citizen

- ✓ Old people are called **senior citizens.**
- ✓ A **law-abiding citizen** is one who never breaks the law.

Criminal

- ✓ A **hardened criminal** is one who continually commits crimes.
- ✓ **Dangerous criminals** may use violence.
- ✓ A **petty criminal** is one who only commits small crimes.

Customer

- ✓ All shops like to **attract customers** to visit them.
- ✓ A **satisfied customer** is one who is happy with what they have bought.
- ✓ If a customer is angry, he or she is an **irate customer.**

Family

- ✓ Parents will **rear their family** which means they look after them and educate them until they leave home.
- ✓ In times of trouble **families stick together**.

- ✓ Children who live with one parent are in a **single-parent family**.
- ✓ Families which have major problems are **dysfunctional families.**
- ✓ A family who sees each other a lot and gets on well can be described as a **close family**.

Fool

- ✓ An **utter fool** is a person who is always stupid.
- ✓ If someone **plays the fool,** they act in a stupid manner.

Friend

- ✓ To **make friends**, is to find and to start to be a friend with someone.
- ✓ If you **lose a friend**, your friendship ceases.
- ✓ An **intimate friend** is one who is very close to you.
- ✓ **Good friends** are always ready to help each other when one of them has a problem.

Immigrant

- ✓ An **illegal immigrant** is one who has entered a country without permission.
- ✓ An **economic immigrant** goes to another country only to earn money.
- ✓ There is a large **immigrant population** in most cities these days.

Leader

- ✓ A **charismatic leader** is one who has a great influence over the people who he or she leads.
- ✓ A **born leader** is a person who leads naturally.

Opponent

- ✓ If you **get the better of an opponent**, you beat her or him.
- ✓ A **worthy opponent** is someone who is equal to your skills.
- ✓ A **formidable opponent** is one which will be a great challenge.

Parents

- ✓ Many children **take after their parents**, meaning they are the same as their Mum and Dad.
- ✓ People who do not look after their children correctly are **unfit parents**.
- ✓ People who are very happy after having a newborn baby are called **proud parents.**
- ✓ **Foster parents** are those who raise children which are not their own.

Patient

- ✓ A doctor **cures patients** and makes them well.
- ✓ Surgeons **operate on patients** in hospital.
- ✓ A **model patient** is one who does exactly what she or he is told to do by doctors.

People

- ✓ **Hard-working people** are those who are not lazy.
- ✓ **Down-trodden people** are those who are not allowed any freedom.
- ✓ If someone has the **voice of the people**, they are important and their ideas express what most people think.
- ✓ A **man / woman of the people** is someone who is loved and respected by many ordinary people.
- ✓ A **people's person** is someone whom many people like very much.

Police

- ✓ The **police force** is the group of police who are in charge of a specific area.
- ✓ If an area is **over-policed,** there are too many police there.
- ✓ **Bent police** are those who are corrupt.
- ✓ **Police on the beat** are those who walk on the street.

Public

- ✓ To **go public**, is to tell many people things which should be secret.
- ✓ If things are **in the public interest**, they need to be known for the public good.
- ✓ A person who is the **public enemy number one** is a person who a whole society is against.

Stranger

- ✓ A **total stranger** is a person who you have never met before.
- ✓ If a person is a **relative stranger**, you haven't seen them for a while.

Student

- ✓ A **promising student** is one who has great potential and is likely to do well.
- ✓ **Conscientious students** take their studies very seriously and work very hard.

Supporter

- ü A **fanatical supporter** is one who is very dedicated and enthusiastic.
- ✓ A **disillusioned supporter** is one who has been disappointed by the team they support.

Team

- ✓ If you are <u>**dropped from the team**</u>, you lose your place in it.
- ✓ The <u>**national team**</u> is one which represents a country.

Writer

- ✓ An <u>**award-winning writer**</u> is one who has won many prizes.
- ✓ A <u>**distinguished writer**</u> is one who is recognised to be very good.

12. Language

Words about Language

Here are some words, which are connected to language and speech:

- ✓ <u>**Linguistics**</u> is the word for the study of language.
- ✓ The <u>**alphabet**</u> is the name for all of the letters in one language.
- ✓ The <u>**vowels**</u> are the letters a, e, i, o and u.
- ✓ <u>**Consonants**</u> are all the letters which are not vowels.
- ✓ A <u>**dialect**</u> is a type of a language which is spoken in one part of a country.
- ✓ <u>**Pronunciation**</u> is the way language is spoken.
- ✓ <u>**Phonetics**</u> is the study of language sounds.
- ✓ <u>**Stress**</u> describes the way certain words are pronounced more forcefully.
- ✓ The <u>**intonation**</u> of your voice is the way the sounds rise and fall.
- ✓ The English <u>**phonetic alphabet**</u> is an alphabet to help you pronounce English words.
- ✓ A person who is <u>**dumb**</u> cannot speak.

- ✓ A person with a **lisp** has difficulty with pronouncing some sounds, usually the -s.
- ✓ **Paralinguistic** signals are all the ways we use to communicate which do not use speech, so with our faces and with our hands.
- ✓ **Speech therapy** is a process, which tries to help and to teach people how to speak.
- ✓ Your **accent** is the way in which you pronounce words.
- ✓ A **diphthong** is the sound of two vowels which when pronounced together make one-sound.
- ✓ To **translate** is to change the meaning of one language into another language.
- ✓ **Slang** is very informal language, for example bloke is slang for a man.
- ✓ Words written in italics are written like this.
- ✓ An **idiom** consists of two or more words, which have one meaning. Very often the meaning cannot be understood from the two words *e.g.* a bad call meaning a bad decision.
- ✓ A **proverb** is a well-known phrase which gives us some advice or describes things which happen in life *e.g.* Too many cooks spoil the broth meaning that if too many people do a job it won't be done properly.

Punctuation

Written language uses punctuation marks to help express the meaning of the written words. Here are the main types of punctuation:

- ✓ . this is a **full stop**. It goes at the end of a sentence.
- ✓ , this is a **comma.** It is used for a pause in a sentence.
- ✓ ? this is **a question mark**. It is used at the end of a question.
- ✓ ! this is an **exclamation mark**. It is used to show emotion in a sentence.

✓ " ... " these are **speech marks**. They go at the start and end of words which are said.

✓ ' this is **an apostrophe.** It is used to show a letter is missing from a contraction.

✓ ; this is a **semicolon**. It is used to separate different ideas or lists.

✓ : this is a **colon.** It is used to show the start of a long list.

✓ (...) these are **brackets**. They are used around words in a sentence which are giving extra information.

— this is **a dash**. It is used to separate parts of a sentence from others.

Grammar terms

Here are some of the words, which are used to describe different aspects of English grammar:

✓ A **clause** is a group of words which includes a verb. A clause is often part of a sentence.

✓ **Compound words** are words which are made of two words but they act like one word, *e.g.* post office, hair-drier

✓ A **collective noun** is one which refers to a group of the things of one type, *e.g.* a group of bees is a swarm.

✓ A **contraction** is when two words are joined, so isn't is the contraction of is not and I'm is the contraction of I am.

✓ The **infinitive** is the basic form of the verb. This can often be found with to.

✓ The **subject** of a sentence is the person who is doing the action of the verb.

✓ The **object** of a sentence is the person who the action is done to.

- ✓ **Irregular** verbs are those which do not end in -ed in the Past Tense.
- ✓ The **passive** is used when the person or thing affected by an action is the subject of the sentence.
- ✓ A **proper noun** is the name of a person or thing, *e.g.* Tom Grant or Taj Mahal.
- ✓ The **modal** verbs are: may, might, can, must, should, would, will and ought.
- ✓ A person's **title** is the word used before their name, *e.g.* Mr, Ms or Dr.
- ✓ A **transitive** verb is a verb, which is followed by an object, *e.g.* "We saw Jaws last night".
- ✓ An **intransitive** verb is one, which never has an obj*ect*, *e.g.* "She cried."

LIST OF IDIOMS AND PROVERBS

A list of idioms can be useful, since the meaning of an idiom cannot be deduced by knowing the meaning of its constituent words.

For example, someone might know perfectly well what a bucket is and also understand the meaning of the verb "to kick", completely; however, unless they had already encountered the meaning of the phrase or were able to tell from the context the phrase appears in, they would not know that *to kick the bucket* is one of the many colourful idioms in the English language meaning *to die*.

English has a tremendous stock of idioms. They can be a source of confusion and frustration to non-native users of the language. When speaking to people who have recently learned English it might aid their ability to comprehend if one avoids idioms. However, most native English speakers have internalized a large repertoire of idioms, which they use often and without thinking much about them so it can be very difficult to censor all idioms from one's speech.

A

Idiom	Meaning
A black look	Giving someone a look of malice; "a dirty look."
A dirty look	A look of disapproval or malice.
A tempest in a teapot (or a storm in a teacup)	A fuss being made about an insignificant matter.
All mouth and trousers	Said of someone who boasts in a macho way but cannot be trusted to achieve what he is clearly fond of talking about.
Arm and a leg (to pay)	An extremely high price.
At the end of the day	A fatalistic phrase suggesting that whatever criticisms or uncertainties arise, the most probable outcome is likely to be x, where x is what has usually happened in the past. Slightly more obscure than "all things considered" and often a tactical way of terminating a discussion or sustained criticism.

B

Idiom	Meaning
Bad	Very good.
Baker's dozen	Thirteen of a particular item.
Ball and chain	(pejorative, or sometimes satirically affectionate).

Bat out of Hell (like a)	Very quickly (also implies haphazardly, frenetically or in a panic).
To bear fruit	To come to profitable conclusion or to produce some worthwhile thing.
Beat a dead horse	Beating a dead horse is to engage in pointless and repetitive discussion. *Beating* is more common in American idiom, while *Flogging a dead horse* is more common in Britain.
Beat around the bush	Procrastinate or hesitate, mainly when one does not want to say something (circumlocution).
Being from Missouri	Skeptical; requiring proof. (The state's unofficial slogan: "Show me" appears on their license plates).
Between a rock and a hard place	Wnen you are "between a rock and a hard place" you are in a very difficult jam, any forseeable resolution of which will not be pleasant. Another common form of this idiom is "between the Devil and the deep blue sea."
Black-hearted	Someone with evil intentions.
Black sheep	An ostracized or ill-fitting member of a family or group. ("Uncle Ned is the black sheep of the family.")
Boot out	To eject a person from a group or society against their wishes.
Born in a barn	Said to someone who fails to close an external door behind them on entering a building, thus causing a discomforting draught. There are regional variations, in Lincolnshire for

	instance, one will hear "Do you come from Barney?" a reference to a windswept fenland village in that English county.
Break a leg	Good luck, especially used to wish luck to stage performers before an opening.
Broken his/her duck	(British), "scored for the first time," or more generally to have avoided complete failure. In British sports slang a "duck's egg" refers to a score of "zero" or "nought". (Similarly "goose eggs" can also mean "00" in American slang.) In the British game of Cricket scoring naught is getting a "duck" and a batter's first run scored is, therefore, "breaking his duck." Generally intended hopefully, as a harbinger of more success to follow. "He's out of his rut and starting to make progress."
Bull in a china shop	A tactless person who upsets others or upsets plans; a very clumsy person.
Burning the candle at both ends	Someone trying to do too much at once, wearing themselves out.
Burning the midnight oil	Studying or working late into, or through, the night.
Bury the hatchet	Make peace with. To end hostilities.
Buy/Bought the farm	To die (possibly a cynical reference to the effect of a life insurance benefits to the beneficiaries; as in "his demise *bought the farm*").
Buying a pig in a poke	To purchase something without inspection, thereby creating an opportunity for fraud. Canonical:

	unethical farmer places a barn-yard cat in a burlap bag (poke) and sells it sight-unseen to another, claiming it contains a piglet. Related to "the cat's out of the bag", below.
By the numbers	To do things precisely as instructed, or as perceived to be instructed.

C

Idiom	Meaning
Call the badger a bishop	This term derives from the practice of badger-baiting, in which a badger is put into a pit and made to fight dogs. To call the badger a bishop is to imply that the badger's overwhelmed condition somehow makes it virtuous, when it is, in fact, just a badger. So, the term means committing the fallacy of projecting virtue on to the oppressed or disadvantaged.
Can of worms	A situation that is hard to deal with, especially one that comes about unexpectedly and intractably. To "open a can of worms" is to get involved with something that is discomforting, hard to resolve, or not easily escaped (closing a container of worms, used as bait by fishermen, generally involves some tricky handling of the wriggling occupants).
Can't see the forest (or wood) for the trees	Losing sight of the big picture by getting mired down in details.
Can't see your nose in front of your face	Being oblivious to something in plain view.

Cat amongst the pigeons	Putting a cat amongst the pigeons involves some, usually premeditated, disruption. Such an act might simply be verbal, cutting across an apparent consensus, but will certainly disturb the equilibrium.
Cat got your tongue?	Asked of someone rendered speechless to emphasize their inability to speak
Cat nap	A short sleep taken during the day. However, this may not necessarily qualify as an "idiom", as the meaning is apparent to some; cats tend to sleep for short intervals (naps) at various times throughout a twenty-four hour period, whereas humans generally sleep for a solid one-third fraction of each day and do not typically "nap" in a catlike manner. Thus, sleeping in this manner is to "nap like a cat", or to take a "cat nap".
Catch 22	A situation from which there is no escape; a problem in which any course of action is likely to result in undesirable consequences. Similar to a "no-win situation" and Hobson's Choice.
Change horses in midstream	Make new plans or choose a new leader in the middle of an important activity. Connotes an unwise, or at best risky, activity.
Close the barn door after the horse gets out	Refers to not taking action until after a problem has already occurred, usually when it's too late and should have been done sooner. "Closing the stable door after the horse has bolted" is the common British variant.

Curiosity killed the cat	As cats are naturally curious, the expression suggests excessive curiosity is not necessarily a good thing, especially where it is not their business.
Cut off your nose to spite your face	To take rash or single-minded action that hurts your own cause in the end. Similar to "throwing the baby out with the bathwater."

D

Idiom	Meaning
Dark horse	A surprise candidate, or competitor; someone who hides their talents or interests. From the metaphor: "He rode in as if on a dark horse in the night" or "No one saw him coming."
Dead and buried	A settled issue. Something no longer needing consideration.
Dead as a doornail	Useless, very distinctly dead. A doornail is the strikeplate for most door knockers. To hold it in place, after it was driven through the door, the pointed end was bent over and buried in the door, to prevent movement. This nail was unrecoverable, so was considered dead to future reclamation, which was apparently common before modern time.
Devil's advocate	To argue a point of view that is not necessarily one's own, but for the sake of fairness. To play "the devil's advocate" in a debate is to ensure that

	some attempt was made to hear a side that might otherwise have gone unrepresented.
dime [for] a dozen	Very common and easy to get; very cheap.
Dog and pony show	A presentation which aims to persuade, generally a marketing presentation, especially one with lots of splashy glitz and little or no real informational content.
Dotting the I's and Crossing the T's	Paying much attention to detail.

E

Idiom	Meaning
Egg on	To provoke or encourage, sometimes in a sarcastic or derisive manner.
Egg on one's face	To be embarrassed.
Elephant in the room	The problem or situation immediately obvious to all but spoken of by none. Usually the topic in question is emotionally charged and so felt by most involved to be best ignored.

F

Idiom	Meaning
Fall on (one's) sword	To take responsibility or blame for a negative outcome, especially if one's own idea To sacrifice oneself.
Feel[ing] blue	Feeling sad, down, or depressed.

A few X short of a Y	Not possessing all of one's mental faculties; *i.e.*, crazy or stupid. These phrases take the form "A few X short of a Y" where X is a common component of Y. In these phrases, Y represents full mental capacity, and the lack of a few X implies a lack of full mental capacity. A few fries short of a Happy Meal. A few sandwiches short of a picnic. Two bricks short of a load. A few syllables short of a Haiku. A couple of cans short of a six-pack. Whimsically derived from "*A few lawnchairs short of a picnic*", with special emphasis on the dearness of syllables (17 altogether) in a Haiku and the sensitivity of the form to nonconformance.
Not the X-est Y in Z	Having comparatively diminished capacities. Similar to "A few X short of a Y", but describing quality rather than quantity and often used for mock-humility. Not the sharpest pencil in the cup. Not the brightest crayon in the box.
First-come, first-served	Indicates a policy of serving clients or customers in the order they arrived without other preferences.
(On a) fishing expedition	Trying to find some evidence of something, often through improper methods. Sometimes used in court.
Five finger discount	To take without paying, to steal, also known as shoplifting.
Full fathoms five	(From Shakespeare, *The Tempest*) Lost deep in the sea.

G

Idiom	Meaning
(bird in a) Gilded cage	In a pleasant situation, but trapped. For example, celebrities that fear the paparazzi are "prisoners in gilded cages," because despite their wealth and fame their every action is under intense scrutiny.
Go with the flow	To conform or go along with whatever happens.
Take it with a grain of salt	To approach a claim with appropriate skepticism.
Graveyard dead	Certainly dead. Emphatically dead.
Gravy Train	An easy or comfortable endeavor.

H

Idiom	Meaning
Have a dog in the fight	To have a stake in, or be exposed to the risks associated with, the outcome of some problem or dispute. Conversely, "I don't have a dog in that fight" is frequently used as a way to beg off and opt out of being expected to assist.
Have one's cake and eat it too	To attempt to get all the positive aspects of something while avoiding any negative but usually occurring aspects.
Herding cats	Trying to elicit coordinated action from a group not inclined to do so. Doing something that is very difficult.

Hit the hay	To go to bed.
Hobson's Choice	A situation from which there is no escape; a problem in which any course of action is likely to result in undesirable consequences. Similar to a "no-win situation" and Catch 22.

I

Idiom	Meaning
In for a penny, in for a pound	Said by someone realising that risks of failure are increasing, but still prepared to press onwards, maintaining their earlier efforts. Similar to the expression "no turning back."
In (out of) the loop	Kept informed (not informed), given feedback.

J

Idiom	Meaning
Juggling picked onions (or frogs)	Carrying out a hazardous or difficult task. Both onions and frogs are slippery and so likely to be hard to juggle with ease.

K

Idiom	Meaning
Keep a stiff upper lip	To exercise self-restraint in the expression of emotion, especially fear or grief
Kick the bucket	To die. Derived from the slaughter of

	pigs, the wooden block a pig was hung from during slaughter was referred to as a buque. Thus in the process of killing the pig, it would inevitably kick it.
Killing two birds with one stone	Completing two tasks with one process or action.
Knock on wood (Knocking on wood)	Knock on something made of wood to keep from having bad luck.

L

Idiom	Meaning
Last straw	A problem or obstacle that may be trivial in itself, but causes cataclysmic failure because it pushes the total array of problems or obstacles to an intolerable level. Also referred to as the Straw that broke the camel's back, after the original proverb: a straw by itself has an insignificant weight, but enough of them together can be a crushing weight.
(the) Lights are on, but no one's home	Said of a person that is lacking intellect and/or sanity, even if they may appear at first to possess full mental faculties. Like "two bricks short of a load", there are endless variations, based around the metaphor of a machine or a system that is not operating as it should ("His elevator doesn't stop at all floors.")
Loan shark	A predatory lender, usually one that charges inordinately high interest.

M

Idiom	Meaning
Make hay	To take advantage of a favourable opportunity. To work diligently toward a goal. Sometimes this idiom appears as "to make hay while the sun shines".
Mind one's p's and q's	Be very careful to behave correctly.
More than one way to kill (or skin) a cat (there is)	Something can be achieved in several different ways.

N

Idiom	Meaning
Nod off	To fall asleep gradually, perhaps reflecting the boredom of a lecture or presentation.
Not playing with a full deck	Someone who is eccentric, mad or wildly unconventional, bordering on crazy. See *Two bricks short of a load* on this page.

O

Idiom	Meaning
Off (or below) the radar	Beyond popular consciousness, less obvious or less mainstream.
Off one's rocker	Crazy
Off the X	Fairly recent slang expression, in which X is replaced by various nouns to make an expression with the general meaning of "great" or "wonderful". (*e.g.* Off the chains, Off the wall, etc.)

On the ball	To be prepared, especially in regards to anticipated future requests or instructions.
On the nose	Exactly correct or correctly.
Out of Sorts	Feeling poorly.
Out of touch	To be unaware of current trends, news, or fashions, especially because of actual physical distance from others.
Over the hill	To be past one's prime, old, a senior citizen. A person has reached his/her peak of physical or employment capabilities and is starting the downhill slide
Over the moon	To be very happy.

P

Idiom	Meaning
Pay through the nose (for something)	Pay too much or a lot of money for something.
Penny wise, pound foolish	Cautious with small amounts of money, but wasteful with large amounts of money.
Pissing in the wind	Continuing with an ineffective action, having no impact on the outcome.
Pissing against the wind	Self-defeat by going against the natural flow of things, against reality.
Pot calling the kettle black	Where person *A* accuses person *B* of something that person *A* is guilty of. The idiom is usually used to imply or accuse someone of hypocrisy.

Pouring cats and dogs	Raining very heavily.
Pulling strings	A reference to those really in power limiting the discretion of those who appear to make decisions, an analogy to those who operate stringed puppets.
Pulling one's leg	Being facetious, or kidding around. Playfully lying.
Pushing up daisies	To be dead. (Example: *He's pushing up daisies.*) This comes from the Western cultural practice of burying the deceased in a cemetery or "memorial park" often with flowers or grass growing at the gravesite.

R

Idiom	Meaning
Reading between the lines	Inferring additional information or nuances not explicitly stated, perhaps revealing a hidden agenda or true motive.
Red light district	An area of town where with a concentration of prostitutes, strip bars, pornography and sex toy shops, and the like.
Red tape	Bureaucratic paperwork, usually in large amounts and being difficult to finish yet seemingly pointless in nature.
Reinvent the wheel	Duplicate a basic method or concept (usually in lieu of pursuing a more original, presumably more worthwhile, goal).
Right under your nose	Something so obvious that it is easily overlooked.

Rob Peter to pay Paul	Solving a problem in a way that leads to a new problem; a quick solution with an obvious drawback.
Rock the boat	Breaking with tradition or going against custom or an apparent
	consensus, possibly with entirely benign motives — but perhaps out of selfishness.
Rooted to the spot	One that has not moved out of the place where the person has been for a long time. Both in physical, and in mental situations.

S

Idiom	Meaning
Set the Thames on fire	Perform an astonishing feat. This phrase is almost invariably used in the negative: "He'll never set the Thames on fire." Latin and German have similar idioms regarding the Tiber and the Rhine, respectively.
To travel by Shank's Pony	To walk
Six feet under	Dead and buried (from a traditional depth for human graves).
Six of one, half a dozen of another	Two things that are essentially the same and so there is no real choice to be made.
Slow as molasses	To work or act in a slow manner.
Soup to nuts	From beginning to end; etymologically, from the first course of a meal (soup) to the last course (nuts).

Sour grapes	To decide that the attainment of something you have been thwarted from getting is not worth it after all and probably inferior in quality anyway. (Aesop's Fables: *The Fox and the Grapes*).
To spin a yarn	To tell a story, especially one with distorted truths or exaggerations.
Spirit of the law	To interpret something as it is meant, not as explicitly stated.
Squaring the circle	Trying to do something which is impossible.
Stalking horse	A political candidate unlikely to succeed against an incumbent, standing to generate an election and to reveal disquiet with the incumbent's recent performance—possibly inducing other competitors for that post to declare their interest.
Start with a clean slate/ sheet (of paper)	To contemplate solving a problem without preconceptions.
Steal someone's thunder	Taking the credit for something positive occasioned largely by someone else.
Stem the tide	To stop or control the growth or increase of something, usually unpleasant.
Stick in the mud	An old fashioned idea or concept, or someone who moves or adapts slowly. Also used to describe a person who does not want to participate in activities suggested by one or more people.

Straw that broke the camel's back	From a proverb about loading up a camel beyond its capacity to move. This is a reference to any process by which cataclysmic failure (a broken back) is achieved by a seemingly inconsequential addition (a single straw). This also gives rise to the phrase "the last straw".
Swan song	A final appearance; a theatrical or dramatic farewell (from a legendary belief that a mute swan would sing its own dirge as it died).
Swim with the fishes	To die, especially to be murdered and have your body disposed of, often in a body of water. (See also "sleep with the fishes"). It's presumed to be a bit of Mafia jargon.
Sword of Damocles	The Sword of Damocles is a frequently used symbolic allusion to this myth, referring to the insecurity felt by those with great power due to the possibility of that power being taken away suddenly, or, more generally, any feeling of impending doom.

T

Idiom	Meaning
Take a flyer	To take a chance or risk.
Take a seat	A command or request to sit down.
Taken to the cleaners	Defrauded, robbed, cheated, conned.
Tall tale	A (sometimes boastful) unrealistic story, often told in a humorous way.

That was then, and this is now	To denote a change between the situation in the past and the current one.
The cat's out of the bag	*To let the cat out of the bag* A secret or hidden thing has been discovered. Related to "buying a pig in a poke", above.
The Powers That Be	Generic term for people who are in charge of something. Often used either derisively or when the actual people are not known. Usually capitalized.
((The) tail that) wag(s) the dog	To note or have an out of porportion impact or influence. "He is addicted to Wikipedia, it's the tail that wags the dog." To note reversal of a typical or expected causality chain, usually in exclamation. "That bird frightened the cat! Doesn't that just wag the dog!"
Three sheets to the wind	Drunk. Usually heavily inebriated.
Throw down the gauntlet	To challenge
To be catty	To be antagonistic, usually applied to women.
To pocket	To attempt to steal by slipping. something unnoticed into a concealed place (pocket, purse, jacket, etc.)
To the letter	To interpret and follow instructions or rules in as literal a manner as possible, doing nothing that one is not explicitly instructed or told to do, often deliberately ignoring the implicit meaning of those instructions or rules.

To turn turtle	To capsize
Toot your own horn/blow your own trumpet	To brag about oneself, often downplaying the contributions of others.
Toe the line	To follow rules and regulations faithfully. To be careful to never commit any transgressions. To conform, particularly to conform to onerous or odious demands through loyalty.
Treading water	Making no progress.
	Not possessing all of one's mental faculties; *i.e.*, crazy or stupid. AKA "two bricks *shy* of a load". The general form "N Xs short of a Y", where N is a small number and X is an item in a set Y, provides endless recognizable variations. Examples: "two chairs short of a set" (*Gilmore Girls*, "Emily in Wonderland"); "One Can Short of a 6 Pack" (Da Yoopers album); "two deuces shy of a deck" (playing cards) (see "Not playing with a full deck").

U

Idiom	Meaning
Under the weather	To be feeling ill.
Up a creek (sometimes, up shit's creek) without a paddle	To be in an untenable position. To have no recourse or satisfactory course of action.

W

Idiom	Meaning
Wake up on the wrong side of the bed	To be very grumpy. Usually used in response to discovering someone is very grumpy. "Whoa! Looks like you woke up on the wrong side of the bed today!
Water under the bridge	Something that has happened in the past and is no longer worth agonizing over. A dismissal of prior offenses or transgressions. Generally said after emotional conflicts.
When the gloves are off	After the polite negotiations have failed, when false posturing is no longer plausible. Similar to "when the chips are down" or "when push comes to shove".
Whole nine yards	The entire amount, everything. Comes from the 9 yard machine gun belts used in some military aircraft during WWII etc. Gunners would say "I gave them (the enemy) the whole nine yards.

English Proverbs

1. "A poor workman blames his tools."
2. "A bird in the hand is worth two in the bush."
3. "Absence makes the heart grow fonder."
4. "A cat may look at a king."
5. "A chain is no stronger than its weakest link."
6. "A coward dies a thousand times before his death. The valiant never taste of death but once."

7. "A creaking door hangs longest." and "A creaking gate hangs long."
8. "Actions speak louder than words."
9. "Advice when most needed is least heeded."
10. "A fool and his money are soon parted."
11. "A fox smells its own lair first." and " A fox smells its own stink first."
12. "A friend in need is a friend indeed."
13. "After a storm comes a calm."
14. "After dinner sit a while, after supper walk a mile."
15. "A good beginning makes a good ending."
16. "A good man in an evil society seems the greatest villain of all."
17. "A good surgeon has an eagle's eye, a lion's heart, and a lady's hand."
18. "A guilty conscience needs no accuser."
19. "A jack of all trades is master of none."
20. "A lie has no legs."
21. "A lie can be halfway around the world before the truth gets its boots on."
22. It's easier to turn falsehood loose than correct it everywhere it runs to.
23. "A little knowledge is dangerous. Drink deep, or taste not the puritan waters."
24. "A little Learning is a dangerous Thing.
25. "All of you that intend to ring, you undertake a dangerous thing."
26. "A merry heart makes a long life."
27. "A miss by an inch is a miss by a mile."
28. "A penny saved is a penny earned."
29. "A penny saved is very grateful."
30. "A person is known by the company he keeps."

31. "A picture is worth a thousand words."
32. "A picture is worth a thousand words, and yet picture books are for infants."
33. "A pot of milk is ruined by a drop of poison."
34. "A rolling stone gathers no moss."
35. "A sound mind in a sound body."
36. "A stitch in time saves nine." This is attributed to Benjamin Franklin under American proverbs.
37. "All cats love fish but hate to get their paws wet."
38. "All flowers are not in one garland."
39. "All frills and no knickers."
40. "All good things come to an end."
41. "All hat and no cattle."
42. "All roads lead to Rome."
43. "All's fair in love and war."
44. "All's well that ends well."
45. "All that glitters is not gold."
46. "All things come to he who waits."
47. "All work and no play makes Jack a dull boy."
48. "An apple a day keeps the doctor away."
49. An Englishman's home is his castle"
50. "An eye for an eye and a tooth for a tooth."
51. "Another man's poison is not necessarily yours."
52. "One man's medicine is another man's poison."
53. "An ounce of prevention is worth a pound of cure."
54. "April showers bring May flowers."
55. "Ask and you shall receive."
56. "Ask me no questions, I'll tell you no lies."
57. "As you make your bed, so you must lie in it."
58. "As you sow, so shall you reap."
59. "A watched kettle never boils."

60. "But an unwatched kettle over boils!"
61. "A woman's work is never done."
62. "A woman needs a man like a fish needs a bicycle."
63. A word to the wise is enough" (or "sufficient.")
64. "A word spoken is past recalling."
65. "Barking dogs seldom bite."
66. "Be careful what you wish for, you might just get it."
67. "Beauty is in the eye of the beholder."
68. "Beauty is only skin deep, but ugly goes straight to the bone."
69. "Beauty may open doors but only virtue enters."
70. "Beer before liquor, you'll never be sicker, but liquor before beer and you're in the clear."
71. "Beggars can't be choosers."
72. "Better to be thought a fool, than to open your mouth and remove all doubt."
73. "Better late than never."
74. "Better safe than sorry."
75. "Better the devil you know than the devil you don't."
76. "Birds of a feather flock together."
77. "Bitter pills may have blessed effects."
78. "Blood is thicker than water."
79. "Blood will out."
80. "Boys will be boys."
81. "Brain is better than brawn."
82. "Bread is the staff of life."
83. "Brevity is the soul of wit."
84. "Butter is gold in the morning, silver at noon, lead at night."
85. "Cast not your pearls before swine."
86. To waste something of value on those who won't or can't appreciate it.

87. "Chance favours the prepared mind."
88. "Cider on beer, never fear; beer upon cider, makes a bad rider."
89. "Close but no cigar."
90. "Close only counts in horseshoes and hand-grenades."
91. "Clothes make(th) the man."
92. "Cobbler, stick to thy last."
93. "Common sense ain't common."
94. "Cowards die many times, but a brave man only dies once."
95. "Cross the stream where it is the shallowest."
96. "Curiosity killed the cat. Satisfaction brought it back, that's why the cat has nine lives."
97. "Cut your coat according to your cloth."
98. "Desperate diseases must have desperate cures."
99. "Desperate times call for desperate measures."
100. "Desperate diseases must have desperate remedies."
101. "Desperate times call for desperate measures."
102. "Different sores must have different salves."
103. "Different strokes for different folks."
104. "Diseases come on horseback, but steal away on foot."
105. "Do as you would be done by."
106. "Do unto others as you would have done to you."
107. "Doctors make the worst patients."
108. "Don't bite the hand that feeds you."
109. "Don't burn your bridges before they're crossed."
110. "Don't burn your bridges behind you."
111. "Don't change horses in midstream."
112. "Don't count your chickens before they're hatched."
113. "Don't cross a bridge until you come to it."
114. "Don't cry over spilt milk."

115. "Don't cut off your nose to spite your face."
116. "Don't have too many irons in the fire."
117. "Don't judge a book by its cover."
118. "Don't look a gift horse in the mouth."
119. "Looking at a horse's mouth is one classic way to judge it's health."
120. "Don't make a mountain out of a molehill."
121. "Don't exaggerate small things."
122. "Don't mend what ain't broken."
123. Alternately, "If it ain't broke, don't fix it."
124. "Don't put all your eggs in one basket."
125. "Don't put the cart before the horse."
126. "Don't shut the barn door after the horse is gone."
127. "Don't spoil the ship for a halfpenny of tar."
128. "Don't use your hairdryer in the shower, you prat"
129. "Don't do something that's just going to get you back."
130. "Don't throw out the baby with the bathwater."
131. "Don't trudge mud into the house of love."
132. "Don't trust the Greek bearing gifts."
133. "Doubt is the beginning, not the end, of wisdom."
134. "Do or die."
135. "Do the thing you fear, the death of fear is certain."
136. "If you were born to be shot, you'll never be hung."
137. "Early bird gets the worm."
138. "Early to bed and early to rise makes a man healthy, wealthy, and wise."
139. "Early to rise early to bed makes a man socialy dead."
140. "Eat to live, don't live to eat."
141. "Eat when you're hungry, and drink when you're dry."
142. "East or West, home is best."
143. "Education is a subversive activity."

144. "Empty barrels make the most sound."
145. "Even a blind squirrel finds a nut once in a while."
146. "Even a worm will turn."
147. "Even a broken clock is right twice a day."
148. "Every cloud has a silver lining." 
149. "Every coin has two sides".
150. "Every day is a new beginning."
151. "Every disease will have its course."
152. "Every dog has its day."
153. "Every man has a price."
154. "Every rule has its exception."
155. "Everything comes to him who waits."
156. "Everything's eventual."
157. "Every why has a wherefore."
158. "Every path has its puddle."
159. "Faith will move mountains."
160. "Faint heart ne'er won fair lady."
161. "Familiarity breeds contempt."
162. "Fine feathers make fine birds."
163. "Fine words butter no parsnips."
164. "First come, first served."
165. "First deserve then desire."
166. "Fool me once, shame on you. Fool me twice, shame on me."
167. "Fools rush in where angels fear to tread."
168. "Forewarned is forearmed."
169. "Fourty Two is the answer."
170. "Fresh pork and new wine kill a man before his time."

171. "Fretting cares make grey hairs."
172. "Friend to all is a friend to none."
173. "Friend in need is a friend indeed."
174. "Garbage in, garbage out."
175. "Give and take is fair play."
176. "Give a dog a bad name and hang him."
177. "Give the Devil his due."
178. "God blesses a drunk."
179. "God cures and the physician takes the fee."
180. "Good eating deserves good drinking."
181. "Good fences make good neighbors."
182. "Good men are scarce."
183. "Good wine needs no bush."
184. "Great minds think alike, but fools seldom differ."
185. "Great oaks from little acorns grow."
186. "Green leaves and brown leaves fall from the same tree."
187. "Grow where you are planted."
188. "Hair of the dog that bit you."
189. "Half a loaf is better than none."
190. "Handsome is as handsome does."
191. "Hang a thief when he's young, and he'll no' steal when he's old."
192. "Happy wife, happy life."
193. "Hard cases make bad law."
194. "Hard words break no bones."
195. "Haste makes waste."
196. "Have not want not." said by Lee Field Walstad."
197. "Hawks will not pick out hawks' eyes."
198. "Health is better than wealth."
199. "Heaven protects children, sailors and drunken men."
200. "Hell hath no fury like a woman scorned."

201. "He goes a'sorrowing who goes a'borrowing."
202. "Help a lame dog over a stile."
203. "He that lives too fast, goes to his grave too soon."
204. "He that will steal an egg will steal an ox."
205. "He who hesitates is lost."
206. "He who laughs last laughs best."
207. "He who laughs last laughs longest."
208. "He who last, lasts, laughs last."
209. "A cobbler formed the shape of shoes on a wooden foot shaped last. If it lasted long he was happy."
210. "He who lives by the sword shall die by the sword."
211. "He who pays the piper calls the tune."
212. "To be able to contol the details of a situation by virtue of being the one who bears the cost or provides for others."
213. "He who sleeps forgets his hunger."
214. "He's all hat and no cattle."
215. "Purely bluster and no substance."
216. "Hindsight is 20/20."
217. "His bark is worse than his bite."
218. "History repeats itself."
219. "History never repeats itself, but it does rhyme." — Mark Twain.
220. "Home is where the heart is."
221. "Home is where you hang your hat."
222. "Honesty is the best policy."
223. "Honey catches more flies than vinegar."
224. "Hope for the best, expect the worst."
225. "Hunger is the best spice."
226. "Hunger is the best sauce."
227. "Hunger makes good kitchen."

228. "Hope is life.", by deadman.
229. "If at first you don't succeed, try, try again."
230. "If at first you don't succeed, try, try again. Then give up, it's no good being pig-headed."
231. "If at first you don't succeed, redefine success."
232. "If at first you don't succeed, give up skydiving."
233. "If at first you don't succeed, try a shorter bungee."
234. "If at first you don't succeed, well, you're about average."
235. "If a thing is worth doing, it's worth doing well."
236. "If it is worth doing, it is worth doing poorly."
237. "If ignorance is bliss, why aren't more people happy?"
238. "If it isn't broke, don't fix it."
239. "If it jams, force it. If it breaks, it probably needed fixing anyway."
240. "If mama ain't happy, ain't nobody happy."
241. "If something can go wrong, it will."
242. "If the cap fits, wear it."
243. "If the shoe fits, wear it."
244. "If wishes were horses, beggars would ride."
245. "If wishes were horses, then beggers would ride, but you better not think about going outside."
246. "If words could only speak, they'd mean even less."
247. "If you buy cheaply, you pay dearly."
248. "If you can't beat them, join them."
249. "If you can't join them, beat them."
250. "If you can't be good, be careful."
251. "If you can't take the heat, get out of the kitchen."
252. "If you don't love yourself with passion, you'll love others with it. Passion is conserved."
253. "If you keep your mouth shut, you won't put your foot in it."

254. "If you want a thing done well, do it yourself."
255. "If you're in a hole, stop digging."
256. "Ignorance is bliss."
257. "In for a penny, in for a pound."
258. "In the land of the blind, the one-eyed man is king."
259. "In the end, a man's motives are second to his accomplishments."
260. "It's a good horse that never stumbles."
261. "It never rains, but it pours."
262. "It's a long lane that has no turning."
263. "It's an ill wind that blows no good."
264. "It's better to give than to receive."
265. "It's better to have loved and lost than never to have loved at all."
266. "It's easy to be wise after the event."
267. "It's never too late to mend."
268. "It's not over till it's over." — Yogi Berra
269. or, "It ain't over till it's over."
270. "It's no use crying over spilt milk."
271. "It's often a person's mouth broke their nose."
272. "It's the early bird that gets the worm."
273. "It's the empty can that makes the most noise."
274. "It's the squeaky wheel that gets the grease."
275. "It pays to pay attention."
276. "It takes all sorts to make a world."
277. or, "It takes all sorts to make the world go round."
278. also, "It takes all kinds to make the world go round."
279. "It takes two to make a quarrel."
280. "It takes two to tango."
281. "It takes two to lie, one to lie and one to listen."

282. "If you dont have anything nice to say, dont say anything at all!"
283. "Jack is as good as his master."
284. "Jack of all trades, master of none."
285. "Jam tomorrow and jam yesterday, but never jam today."
286. "Jove but laughs at lover's perjury."
287. "Judge not, lest ye be judged."
288. "Just do it!"
289. "Keep a thing seven years and you will always find a use for it."
290. "Keep no more cats than catch mice."
291. "Kill not the goose that laid the golden egg."
292. "Kill two birds with one stone."
293. "Knock and the door will be opened unto you."
294. "Laughter is the best medicine."
295. "Laughter is the shortest distance between two people."
296. "Learn to walk before you run."
297. "Let him who is without sin cast the first stone."
298. "Let sleeping dogs lie."
299. "Lie down with dogs, wake up with fleas."
300. "Like cures like."
301. "Like father like son."
302. "Like water off a duck's back."
303. "Little by little and bit by bit."
304. "Little enemies and little wounds must not be despised."
305. "Liquor before beer and you're in the clear. Beer before liquor and you'll never be sicker."
306. "Long absent, soon forgotten."
307. "Look after the pennies and the pounds will look after themselves."
308. "Look before you leap."

309. "Loose lips sink ships."
310. "Love is blind."
311. "Life begins at forty."
312. "Live and let die."
313. "Live and let Live."
314. "Life's a bitch and then you die."
315. "Life's a bitch and then you marry one."
316. "Life's a bleach and then you dye."
317. "Make hay while the sun shines."
318. "Make love not war."
319. "Make love like war."
320. "Making a rod for your own back."
321. "Man with four balls can't walk."
322. "Many hands make light work."
323. "Many a mickle makes a muckle."
324. "Many a true word is spoken in jest."
325. "Measure twice, cut once."
326. "Misery loves company."
327. "Money for old rope."
328. "Money makes the mare go."
329. "Money makes the world go around."
330. "Money talks."
331. "Money talks, bullshit walks."
332. "More haste, less speed."
333. "Mouth is in gear, brain is in neutral."
334. "Nature abhors a vacuum."
335. "Nature, time, and patience are three great physicians."
336. "Necessity is the mother of all invention."
337. "Never judge the book by it's cover."
338. "Not to be taken by it's look on the surface."
339. "Never, Never... allow anyone to persuade you to suspend your common sense."

340. "Never rub another man Rhubarb."
341. "Never put off till (until) tomorrow what you can do today."
342. "Never do today what you can put off till (until) tomorrow."
343. "It was probably a waste of time anyway."
344. "Never trouble trouble until trouble troubles you."
345. "New brooms sweep clear."
346. "New broom sweeps clean."
347. "Noblesse oblige."
348. "No cows, no cares."
349. "No gain without pain."
350. "No hoof, no horse."
351. "No man can serve two masters."
352. "No man is content with his lot."
353. "No man is an island"
354. "No news is good news."
355. "No pain, no gain."
356. "No pain, no injury."
357. "No time to waste like the present."
358. "Nothing ventured, nothing gained."
359. "Nothing succeeds like success."
360. "Old is gold."
361. "Once bitten, twice shy."
362. "One doctor makes work for another."
363. "One good turn deserves another."
364. "One man's trash is another man's treasure."
365. "One man's meat is another's poison."
366. "Only two things in life are certain; death and taxes."
367. "Out of sight, out of mind."
368. "Paddle your own canoe."

369. "Pain is only weakness leaving the body."
370. "Patience is a virtue."
371. "Penny wise, pound foolish."
372. "People who live in glass houses shouldn't throw stones."
373. "Power corrupts; absolute power corrupts absolutely."
374. "Power attracts the corruptible." -from Dune series, Frank Herbert.
375. "Practice makes perfect."
376. "Practice makes permanent."
377. "Rats desert a sinking ship."
378. "Red sky at night: shepherd's delight. Red sky in the morning: shepherd's warning."
379. "Rolling stone gathers no moss."
380. "Rome wasn't built in a day."
381. "Rules are made to be broken."
382. "Scratch my back and i will scratch yours".
383. "Seek and ye shall find."
384. Set a thief to catch a thief.
385. "Smile, and the world smiles with you. Cry, and you cry alone."
386. "Sometimes people who live in glass houses throw stones because their windows are painted"-James Finstrom.
387. "Starve a fever, feed a cold."
388. "Still waters are the deepest."
389. "Stolen fruit is sweet."
390. "Sticks and stones may break my bones but words will never hurt me."
391. "Still waters run deep."
392. "Strike while the iron is hot."
393. Seize the moment. Take the opportunity now; don't waste it.

394. "Try not to become a man of success but a man of value."
395. "Talk is cheap."
396. "Talk of the devil - and the devil appears."
397. "Talk the hind legs off a donkey."
398. "Talking a mile a minute."
399. "The best things in life are free."
400. "The coat makes the man."
401. "The cure is worse than the disease."
402. "The early bird gets the worm."
403. "The early bird gets the worm, but the second mouse gets the cheese."
404. "The end justifies the means."
405. "The English are a nation of shopkeepers" (attributed to Napoleon).
406. "The first step to health is to know that we are sick."
407. "The grass is always greener on the other side of the fence."
408. "The head and feet keep warm, the rest will take no harm."
409. "The more things change, the more they stay the same."
410. "The nail that sticks out gets pounded."
411. "The only stupid question is the one that is not asked."
412. "The opera ain't over until the fat lady sings."
413. "The pitcher goes so often to the well that it comes home broken at last."
414. "The proof of the pudding is in the eating."
415. "The road to hell is paved with good intentions."
416. "The spirit is willing but the flesh is weak."
417. "The squeaky wheel gets the grease."
418. "The start of a journey should never be mistaken for success."

419. "The third time someone tries to put a saddle on you, you should admit you're a horse."
420. "The truth shall set you free," or "The truth will set you free."
421. "The wish is father to the thought."
422. "There are no small parts, only small actors."
423. "There are too many chiefs and not enough Indians."
424. "There's always a calm before a storm."—Shanth.
425. "There's always a deep breath before a plunge."
426. "There's many a slip 'twixt the cup and the lip."
427. "There's more than one way to skin a cat."
428. "There's no accounting for taste."
429. "There's no arguing with the barrel of a gun."
430. "The beauty of things lies in the mind that contemplates it."
431. "There's no place like home."
432. "There's no time like the present."
433. "Think before you speak."
434. "Think globally, act locally."
435. "Those who live in glass houses shouldn't throw stones."
436. "Time flies when you're having fun."
437. "Time flies like an arrow, fruit flies like a banana."—Groucho Marx.
438. "Time is money."
439. "Time is of the esscence."
440. "This too, shall pass."
441. "To each his own."
442. "To err is human; to forgive is divine." (Pope, *Essay on Criticism*)
443. "To kill two birds with one stone."
444. "Tomorrow is another day."
445. "Too many chiefs and not enough indians."

446. "Too many cooks spoil the broth."
447. "Trouble shared is trouble halved."
448. "Truth is stranger than fiction."
449. "Truth will out."
450. "Two's company, three's a crowd."
451. "Two heads are better than one."
452. "Two things prolong your life: A quiet heart and a loving wife."
453. "Two wrongs don't make a right."
454. "Two wrongs don't make a right, but three lefts do."
455. "Treat them mean, keep them keen."
456. "Up a creek without a paddle."
457. "Variety is the spice of life."
458. "Waste not, want not."
459. "We all make mistakes."
460. "We are all in this together."
461. "We must take the bad with the good."
462. "That which does not kill you, makes you stronger."
463. "What goes around comes around."
464. "What goes up must come down."
465. "What's sauce for the goose is sauce for the gander."
466. "When the cat's away, the mice will play."
467. "When the going gets tough, the tough get going."
468. "When you hear hoofbeats, think horses, not zebras."
469. "When your only tool is a hammer, every problem looks like a nail."
470. "Where one door shuts, another opens."
471. "Where there's a will there's a way."
472. "Where's there's muck, there's money."
473. "While the cat is away, the mice will play."
474. "While there's life, there's hope."
475. "Whiskey on beer, never fear. Beer on whiskey, mighty risky."

476. “Who keeps company with the wolves, will learn to howl.”
477. “Whom we love best, to them we can say the least.”
478. “Why have a dog and bark yourself?”
479. “Why pay for the cow when the milk is free?”
480. “”Wide ears and short tongue are the best.”
481. “Winners never cheat and cheaters never win.”
482. “Without sleep, no health.”
483. “You are responsible for you.”
484. “You can catch more flies with honey than with vinegar.”
485. “You can lead (take) a horse to water but you can’t make it drink.”
486. “You can’t free a fish from water.”
487. “You can’t have it both ways.”
488. “You can’t judge a book by its cover.”
489. “You can’t make an omelette without breaking eggs.”
490. “You can’t make a silk purse out of a sow’s ear.”
491. “You can’t milk a cow with your hands in your pants.”
492. “You can’t run with the hare and hunt with the hounds.”
493. “You can’t teach an old dog new tricks.”
494. “You can’t teach grandma to suck eggs.”
495. “You can’t teach grandpa to suck eggs.”
496. “You can’t tell a book by its cover.”
497. “You have to crawl before you can walk.”
498. “You’ll always miss 100% of the [basketball] shots you don’t take.”
499. “You need to bait the hook to catch the fish.”

ADVANCED V( **FOR USE**

abase (v.) - to lower, demean, degrade

abate (v.) - to lessen, to reduce in severity

abbreviate (v.) - to shorten, reduce

abduct (v.) - to kidnap

aberration (n.) - a deviation from the expected course

abhor (v.) - to hate, loathe

abide (v.) - to put up with, tolerate

abject (adj.) - of the most miserable or contemptible kind

abort (v.) - to give up unfinished

abridge (v.) - to shorten, cut down

abrogate (v.) - to abolish, often by authority

abscond (v.) - to sneak away and hide

abundant (adj.) - in great numbers

accede (v.) - to agree

accentuate (v.) - to emphasize, to highlight

accommodating (adj.) - obliging, helpful

accost (v.) - to approach or confront aggressively

acumen (n.) - keen insight

acute (adj.) - sharp, severe

affable (adj.) - friendly, amiable

affluent (adj.) - rich, wealthy

aggrandize (v.) - to increase or make greater

aggregate (v.) - to gather, amass

aghast (adj.) - struck by amazement or terror

agoraphobia (n.) - an abnormal fear of open or public places

akimbo (adj.) - with hands on hips and elbows extending outward

alacrity (n.) - speed, readiness

algid (adj.) - frigid, cold

allay (v.) - to sooth, assuage

alleviate (v.) - to relieve

aloof (adj.) - reserved, distant

altercation (n.) - an argument, dispute

amalgamation (n.) - a union, a merger

ambivalent (adj.) - having contradictory feelings

amble (v.) - to stroll, walk

ameliorate (v.) - to improve, to make better

amend (v.) - to change for the better, improve

amiable (adj.) - friendly, affable

amorous (adj.) - relating to or showing love

amorphous (adj.) - without shape or borders

anomaly (n.) - something that does not fit into the normal order

antechamber (n.) - a waiting room

anxiety (n.) - uneasiness

aphorism (n.) - a short saying

apocalypse (n.) - total devastation, the end of the world

apparitional (adj.) - ghostly, spectral

arbitrator (n.) - one who settles controversy between two sides

ascetic (n.) - one who practices restraint as a means of self-discipline, usually religious

assuage (v.) - to ease, pacify

atone (v.) - to apologize, make amends

audacious (adj.) - excessively bold

augment (v.) - to increase or make larger

austere (adj.) - very bare, bleak, simple

baleful (adj.) - harmful, threatening

bard (n.) - a poet, often a singer as well

battery (n.) - an assault or an array of similar things intended for use together

belligerent (adj.) - contentious, ready to fight

benevolent (adj.) - kind, good, caring

benign (adj.) - non-threatening, innocuous

berate (v.) - to scold severely

bereft (adj.) - without, devoid of

bide (v.) - to wait, or remain in a condition

bilk (v.) - to cheat, to swindle

blandish (v.) - to coax through flattery

bloated (adj.) - swollen, bigger than desired

boisterous (adj.) - loud, energetic

bourgeois (adj.) - middle class

brash (adj.) - hasty or lacking in sensitivity

brazen (adj.) - excessively bold, brash

brumal (adj.) - wintry, relating to winter

brusque (adj.) - short, abrupt, dismissive

buffet (n.) - a spread of food involving choices

buffet (v.) - to hit or strike

burgeon (v.) - to come forth, blossom

cacophony (n.) - noise, discordant sound

cadence (n.) - rhythm

cajole (v.) - to urge, coax

callous (adj.) - harsh, cold, unfeeling

calumny (n.) - an attempt to defame another's reputation

camaraderie (n.) - cheerful unity among a group

canvas (n.) - a piece of cloth on which an artist paints

capricious (adj.) - impulsive, unpredictable, subject to whim

captivate (v.) - to hold the interest of, to gain the attention of

carouse (v.) - to revel, to party

cavity (n.) - a hole

cavort (v.) - to frolic, leap, prance

celestial (adj.) - relating to the sky or the heavens

chastise (v.) - to criticize, to scold

choreographed (adj.) - arranged, as in dance

circumlocution (n.) - indirect language

circumspect (adj.) - cautious
clairvoyant (adj.) - able to see things that others cannot
claustrophobia (n.) - an abnormal fear of closed or crowded spaces
cliché (n.) - a trite, overused expression
coalesce (v.) - to combine into one
cogent (adj.) - intelligent, viable
collusion (n.) - a conspiracy, a secret agreement
colossus (n.) - an enormous structure
comatose (adj.) - lethargic
commendable (adj.) - worthy of praise
commodious (adj.) - spacious, roomy
compel (v.) - to force
complicit (adj.) - being an accomplice in a wrongful act
compliment (n.) - an expression of esteem or approval
concede (v.) - to give in, to accept
conciliatory (adj.) - agreeable, friendly
concoct (v.) - to make up or invent
concord (n.) - agreement
conduit (n.) - a pipe, passage, channel
confluence (n.) - a convergence, a coming together
confound (v.) - to frustrate
connotation (n.) - a meaning or association suggested by a word beyond its definition
contusion (n.) - bruise, injury
convalescence (n.) - the gradual return to health after illness
copious (adj.) - abundant, plentiful
corpulent (adj.) - very fat
cosmopolitan (adj.) - worldly, sophisticated
credulity (n.) - readiness to believe
cursory (adj.) - brief to the point of being superficial

daft (adj.) - insane, foolish
daunting (adj.) - intimidating
dearth (n.) - a lack, scarcity
defame (v.) - to destroy the reputation of
deft (adj.) - skilled, adept
defunct (adj.) - no longer used or existing
deleterious (adj.) - harmful
delude (v.) - to deceive, to mislead
deluge (n.) - a great flood or something that overwhelms like a flood
derelict (adj.) - run-down, abandoned
desolate (adj.) - deserted, lifeless
despondent (adj.) - discouraged, hopeless, depressed
destitute (adj.) - impoverished
diaphanous (adj.) - transparent, light, airy
dictate (v.) - to pronounce, command, prescribe
differentiate (v.) - to distinguish, to make different
dilapidated (adj.) - in a state of disrepair
diligent (adj.) - careful, showing care
diminish (v.) - to decrease or make smaller
diminutive (adj.) - miniature, small
discreet (adj.) - prudent or inconspicuous
discrete (adj.) - separate, distinct, individual
disparage (v.) - to criticize, degrade, belittle
dissonance (n.) - lack of harmony or agreement
divergent (adj.) - different, deviating, contrary
diverse (adj.) - varied
divisive (adj.) - causing conflict, opposition
domicile (n.) - a residence, a home
doppelganger (n.) - a ghostly double of a living person
douse (v.) - to drench, saturate

dutiful (adj.) - careful to fulfill obligations
dynamic (adj.) - characterized by continuous change or activity
elocution (n.) - the art of public speaking
elucidate (v.) - to clarify
empathetic (adj.) - feeling another's pain as one's own
empathy (n.) - the experience of another's feelings as one's own
enervate (v.) - to weaken, make weary
enervated (adj.) - lacking energy, weakened, exhausted
entity (n.) - something that exists as a discrete unit
entomology (n.) - the study of insects
envious (adj.) - jealous
erect (v.) - to construct, to raise
erroneous (adj.) - mistaken, incorrect
espouse (v.) - to support, or to marry
espy (v.)– - catch sight of, glimpse
ethereal (adj.) - heavenly, exceptionally delicate or refined
euphoric (adj.) - elated, overjoyed
exacerbate (v.) - to make more violent, intense
excursion (n.) - a trip, an outing
exemplary (adj.) - serving as an example
exigent (adj.) - critical, urgent
existential (adj.) - relating to existence
exorbitant (adj.) - excessive
extol (v.) - to praise
extravagant (adj.) - excessive, over-the-top
fabricate (v.) - to invent, make-up, concoct
fabulist (n.) - a teller of fables; a liar
facile (adj.) - easy
fallacious (adj.) - incorrect, misleading
familial (adj.) - relating to family

fatuous (adj.) - silly, foolish
fecund (adj.) - fertile, fruitful
feign (v.) - to fake or pretend to
feral (adj.) - savage, wild, untamed
fetter (v.) - to restrain, chain, tie
fey (adj.) - magical
fickle (adj.) - characterized by changeableness, whimsical
figurative (adj.) - symbolic
firmament (n.) - the sky, the heavens
flabbergasted (adj.) - astounded, stupefied
flaccid (adj.) - limp
flattery (n.) - compliments, sycophancy
flout (v.) - to scorn, ignore, show contempt for
fluctuate (v.) - to vary irregularly
flux (n.) - a state of constant change or a flow
forage (v.) - to rummage, scavenge, graze for food
forestall (v.) - to delay, impede
forlorn (adj.) - lonely, hopeless
formidable (adj.) - arousing fear or alarm
forsake (v.) - to abandon, forget
fortify (v.) - to strengthen
fortitude (n.) - strength, bravery
fortuitous (adj.) - lucky, occurring by chance
foster (v.) - to stimulate, promote, encourage
frenetic (adj.) - frenzied, hectic, frantic
gape (v.) - to open the mouth and stare stupidly
gay (adj.) - happy, cheery, or homosexual
gluttonous (adj.) - insatiable in appetite
goad (v.) - to urge, to provoke into action
gourmand (n.) - one who likes eating and drinking
grandiose (adj.) - extraordinary, grand in scope

gregarious (adj.) - sociable, outgoing
grotto (n.) - a small cave or cavern
guile (n.) - deceitful actions or behavior
hail (v.) - to come from
hapless (adj.) - unlucky
harmony (n.) - agreement, often of sound
harrowing (adj.) - agonizing, distressing
hedonist (n.) - one whose primary pursuit is pleasure
henchman (n.) - a trusted follower, goon
hiatus (n.) - an interruption in continuity, a break
hiemal (adj.) - wintry, relating to winter
hierarchy (n.) - a ranking system of groups or individuals
histrionic (adj.) - excessively dramatic or emotional
idolatrous (adj.) - worshiping excessively an object or person
illusory (adj.) - deceptive, produced by an illusion
immaculate (adj.) - impeccably clean, spotless, pure
immutable (adj.) - not susceptible to change
impecunious (adj.) - excessively poor
impervious (adj.) - unable to be penetrated, unaffected
impudent (adj.) - rude, improper
incessant (adj.) - without interruption
incisive (adj.) - clear, sharp, direct
inclement (adj.) - stormy, bad, severe
inclination (n.) - a tendency, propensity
indictment (n.) - accusation of wrongdoing
indignation (n.) - anger due to an unfair situation
inextricable (adj.) - hopelessly confused or tangled
infuse (v.) - to inject
ingenious (adj.) - marked by special intelligence
inimical (adj.) - hostile, threatening
iniquity (n.) - a wicked act, a sin

innate (adj.) - inborn, native, inherent
innocuous (adj.) - harmless
inquisitor (n.) - someone who asks questions or makes an inquiry
inundate (v.) - to flood
invariable (adj.) - not susceptible to change
invective (n.) - a verbal attack
inveterate (adj.) - habitual, natural
irascible (adj.) - easily angered
jubilant (adj.) - joyful, happy
judicious (adj.) - of sound judgment
juvenile (adj.) - young or immature
juxtapose (v.) - to put next to each other
labyrinthine (adj.) - intricate, maze-like
laceration (n.) - a cut, a rip
lachrymose (adj.) - tearful
latent (adj.) - present but hidden
laud (v.) - to applaud or praise
laudatory (adj.) - admiring, praising
lavish (adj.) - extravagant
lethargic (adj.) - sluggish, weary, apathetic
lewd (adj.) - vulgar, offensive, rude
libel (n.) - a statement that gives an unjust or unfavorable representation of a person or thing
licentious (adj.) - amoral, lawless, lewd
limber (adj.) - bending or flexing readily, pliable
limpid (adj.) - clear, easily understood
linchpin (n.) - something that holds separate things together
lithe (adj.) - graceful, flexible, supple
loquacious (adj.) - talkative
lull (n.) - a relatively calm interval, as in a storm

luminescence (n.) - light from non-thermal sources

magnanimous (adj.) - generous, noble

malaise (n.) - vague feeling of discomfort

malevolent (adj.) - having intent to harm others

malicious (adj.) - malevolent, harmful

malign (v.) - to slander, to smear, to libel, to defame, to speak evil of

malleable (adj.) - easily shaped or formed

mandatory (adj.) - required, not optional

manifest (v.) - to show clearly

manifold (adj.) - many

masticate (v.) - to chew

matrimony (n.) - marriage

maudlin (adj.) - sentimental

maxim (n.) - a common saying of advice or virtue

meager (adj.) - lacking in quality stature

mediate (v.) - to intervene, to arbitrate, to sort out

melodramatic (adj.) - exaggeratedly emotional or sentimental; histrionic

mendacious (adj.) - inclined to lie or mislead

mercurial (adj.) - quick and changeable in temperament

meritorious (adj.) - deserving of praise or merit

metamorphosis (n.) - a change of form, shape, substance

mimic (v.) - to imitate, to copy

misogyny (n.) - hatred of women

modicum (n.) - a small amount of something

mollify (v.) - to soften in temper

monogamy (n.) - having only one spouse at a time

mores (n.) - moral attitudes

morose (adj.) - gloomy or sullen

munificent (adj.) - generous, benevolent

mutability (n.) - capability of change
myopic (adj.) - short-sighted
myriad (adj.) - consisting of a very great number
narrate (v.) - to tell a story
nebulous (adj.) - indistinct, hazy
nefarious (adj.) - horribly villainous
neologism (n.) - the creation of new words, or a new word
neonate (n.) - a newborn baby
noisome (adj.) - foul, offensive, particularly to the sense of smell
notoriety (n.) - infamy, known in bad regard
novel (adj.) - strikingly new, unusual, or different
noxious (adj.) - harmful, toxic
obdurate (adj.) - unyielding to persuasion or moral influences
obfuscate (v.) - to render incomprehensible
obsequious (adj.) - excessively compliant or submissive
odious (adj.) - meriting strong displeasure
officious (adj.) - offering unwanted help or service
olfactory (adj.) - relating to the sense of smell
ominous (adj.) - foreboding or foreshadowing evil, portentous
oration (n.) - a dignified and formal speech
ostracize (v.) - to exclude from a community
pacify (v.) - to sooth, ease
paragon (n.) - model of perfection
pariah (n.) - an outcast
parody (n.) - a satirical imitation
patent (adj.) - clear, apparent
pedagogue (n.) - a schoolteacher
pellucid (adj.) - clear
penchant (n.) - a tendency, partiality, preference
peregrinate (v.) - to travel from place to place on foot

perfunctory (adj.) - showing little enthusiasm, done as duty

permeate (v.) - to spread out, to pervade

persevere (v.) - to persist, remain constant

pertinacious (adj.) - stubbornly persistent, holding to a belief or position

peruse (v.) - to examine carefully

pervasive (adj.) - to spread throughout

petulance (n.) - irritability, impoliteness

physiognomy (n.) - the art of judging human character from facial features

pique (v.) - to provoke or to cause indignation

pithy (adj.) - succinctly meaningful

pittance (n.)- - very small amount

placate (v.) - to soothe, appease

placid (adj.) - calm, tranquil

plethora (n.) - a great number, an abundance

pliable (adj.) - flexible, bendable

poach (v.) - to hunt or fish illegally

poised (adj.) - balanced, readied

polygamy (n.) - having more than one spouse at a time

portentous (adj.) - foreboding or foreshadowing evil, ominous

portly (adj.) - fat, chubby, round

precarious (adj.) - dangerously lacking in security or stability

predestination (n.) - the concept of destiny or fate

premonition (n.) - a presentiment of the future

preponderance (n.) - a great amount or frequency

presage (n.) - an omen

prestidigitation (n.) - a sleight of hand

presumptuous (adj.) - disrespectfully bold

profane (adj.) - indecent, blasphemous

profuse (adj.) - abundant, lavish, prolific

propensity (n.) - an inclination, preference

propriety (n.) - decency, state of being proper

protean (adj.) - readily taking on various shapes or forms

prudent (adj.) - cautious, careful

puerile (adj.) - immature

pugnacious (adj.) - belligerent

pulchritude (n.) - physical beauty

punctilious (adj.) - eager to follow rules

pungent (adj.) - having a sharp, strong quality especially related to smell

purport (v.) - to present an intention that is often FALSE

putrid (adj.) - rotten, rancid, foul

quaint (adj.) - old-fashioned

quid pro - (n., latin) – a mutually beneficial exchange

quotidian (adj.) - daily, everyday

radiant (adj.) - bright, beaming

rancid (adj.) - rotten, spoiled, disgusting in smell or taste

ratiocinate (v.) - to think, contemplate

raze (v.) - to demolish

recalcitrant (adj.) - defiant

recalibrate (v.) - to readjust or make corrections to

recapitulate (v.) - to repeat, reiterate

rectify (v.) - to set right, correct

redact (v.) - to revise, edit

redoubtable (adj.) - formidable, commanding respect

redress (v.) - to set right or remedy

reel (v.) - to be thrown off balance or feel dizzy

refrain (v.) - to hold oneself back, forbear

reiterate (v.) - to repeat

relish (v.) - to take zestful pleasure in, enjoy the flavor of

remiss (adj.) - negligent, exhibiting carelessness

render (v.) - to say, or to make

renovate (v.) - to restore, return to original state

repose (n.) - rest, sleep

reprehensible (adj.) - deserving criticism

repudiate (v.) - to reject, turn down

repulse (v.) - to cause disgust or distaste, or to drive back, repel

requisition (n.) - a demand for goods, often by an authority

restitution (n.) - compensation, reimbursement

retaliation (n.) - revenge, punishment

retract (v.) - withdraw

retribution (n.) - vengeance, revenge, payback

revel (v.) - to enjoy

rife (adj.) - abundant

ruddy (adj.) - having a healthy, reddish color

ruse (n.) - a trick

rustic (adj.) - relating to country life

saccharine (adj.) - overly sweet

sacrosanct (adj.) - sacred, holy

sagacious (adj.) - shrewd, showing sound judgment

salient (adj.) - significant, conspicuous

salutation (n.) - a greeting

sanguine (adj.) - cheery, optimistic, hopeful

sate (v.) - to satisfy (an appetite) fully.

satiate (v.) - to satisfy excessively

savor (v.) - to appreciate fully, enjoy

scathing (adj.) - hurtful, critical

scourge (n.) - a plague

scurrilous (adj.) - crude, vulgar

sedate (v.) - to calm, soothe

sedentary (adj.) - sitting

seer (n.) - a fortune teller

seminal (adj.) - original, ground-breaking

serendipity (n.) - the act of finding things not sought, luck

slander (n.) - a FALSE statement to damage the reputation of another

sobriety (n.) - moderation from excess, calm, tranquility

somnolent (adj.) - sleepy

soothsayer (n.) - a fortune teller

sordid (adj.) - dirty

spectral (adj.) - ghostly

spurious (adj.) - FALSE but intended to seem believable or possible

stagnant (adj.) - still, not flowing

stagnate (v.) - to be idle, to be still

static (adj.) - not moving, being at rest

steadfast (adj.) - fixed or unchanging

strenuous (adj.) - requiring tremendous strength or energy

strife (n.) - conflict

stupefy (v.) - to astound

submissive (adj.) - easily yielding to authority

subsist (v.) - to live, exist

succinct (adj.) - marked by compact precision

suffice (v.) - to meet needs

supplant (v.) - to displace and substitute for another

surfeit (n.) - an excess, a surplus, an overabundance

surmise (v.) - to guess, infer, suppose

surreptitious (adj.) - done in a secret, or stealthy way

swarthy (adj.) - of dark color or complexion

sybarite (n.) - someone devoted to pleasure and luxury, a voluptuary

sycophant (n.) - a self-serving flatterer

sympathetic (adj.) - compassionate

sympathy (n.) - an expression of pity for another, compassion

synopsis (n.) - a summary

taciturn (adj.) - not inclined to talk

tantamount (adj.) - equivalent in value or significance

tedious (adj.) - boring, dull

telepathic (adj.) - capable of reading minds

tenuous (adj.) - having little substance or strength

terrestrial (adj.) - relating to the land

terse (adj.) - abrupt, short, brief

timorous (adj.) - fearful, timid

tome (n.) - a large book

toothsome (adj.) - delicious, luscious

torpid (adj.) - lazy, lethargic, moving slowly

torrid (adj.) - giving off intense heat, passionate

tortuous (adj.) - winding, twisted

tragedy (n.) - a disastrous event, or a work of art in which the hero meets a terrible fate

tranquil (adj.) - calm, serene, peaceful

travesty (n.) - a grossly inferior imitation

trek (v.) - to walk, travel by foot

trite (adj.) - overused, hackneyed

truculent (adj.) - eager to fight, violent

ubiquitous (adj.) - existing everywhere, widespread

ultimate (n.) - the last part, or a fundamental element

umbrage (n.) - anger, offense, resentment

uncanny (adj.) - of supernatural character or origin

undulate (v.) - to move in a smooth wavelike motion

uniform (adj.) - unvarying, conforming to one principle

unilateral (adj.) - having only one side

unique (adj.) - being the only one of its kind

upbraid (v.) - to criticize, scold, reproach

vacillate (v.) - to sway from one side to another

variance (n.) - a difference between what is expected and what actually occurs

variegate (v.) - to diversify

vast (adj.) - enormous, immense

veneer (n.) - a superficial or deceptively attractive appearance, façade

veracious (adj.) - honest, truthful

verbose (adj.) - wordy

vicarious (adj.) - experienced through another's actions

vicissitudes (n.) - the unexpected changes and shifts often encountered in one's life

vigour (n.) - vitality and energy, vim.

vim (n.) - and energy, vigour.

vivacious (adj.) - lively, spirited, full of life

vocation (n.) - one's work or professional calling

volition (n.) - a conscious choice or decision

voluminous (adj.) - large, ample

voluptuary (n.) - someone devoted to sensory pleasure and luxury, a sybarite

wane (v.) - to decrease gradually in size or degree

wax (v.) - to increase gradually in size or degree

weather (v.) - to withstand or survive a situation

whet (v.) - to make more keen, stimulate

winsome (adj.) - charming, attractive

Zeitgeist (n.) - the spirit of the time

SECTION 4—CONVERSATIONS

Greetings

Hello and goodbye

Here are common ways of saying hello and goodbye:

Hi.
Hiya.
Hello.
Good morning.
Morning.
Goodbye.
Bye.
See you.
See you later.
Cheerio.
Catch you later.
I must go, bye.
Here are some more formal ways of saying hello:
How do you do?
Pleased to meet you.

Asking people how they are:

When we say hello we also ask how people are. Here are the ways we do this:

Hi, how are you?
Fine thanks, and you?
Fine.
Hi John, how are you?
Not too bad, thanks, and you?
I'm OK, thanks.

Introducing yourself to people you do not know

- Hi, I'm Andrew.
Pleased to meet you Andrew, I'm Joe.
- Hello, my name's Chris, and yours?
I'm Peter.
- Are you Joanna?
Yes, that's right and you?
I'm Tricia.

About you

Here is a list of common questions.

Name?
What's your name? **I'm... / My name is...**

Country?
Where are you from? **I'm (from)...**
What's your nationality? **I'm...**

Live?
Where do you live? **I live in...**

Age?
How old are you? **I'm...**

Married?
Are you married or single? **I'm...**

Likes?
What are your hobbies? **They are...**
What do you like doing? **I like...**

Phone number?
What's your phone number? **It's...**

Job?
What do you do? **I'm a**...
What's your job? **I'm a**...

E-mail?
What's your e-mail address? **It's**...

Birthday?
When's your birthday? **It's on**...

Height?
How tall are you? **I'm**...

Favourite film?
What's your favourite film? **It's**...

Favourite music?
What music do you like? **I like**...

Conversation

How to offer/refuse
Would you like a Coke? - Yes, I'd love to.
Yes, please.
No, thank you.
Understanding
I didn't quite get that.
Can you repeat that, please?
I didn't understand you.
How to ask/argue
Are you saying that ...?
Can you explain that?
Sorry to interrupt you, ...
I actually wanted to say that ...

Well, ...
I don't think so.
I'm sure that ...
There's nothing more to say.
Obviously I don't need to say that ...
General
Besides ...
It doesn't matter.
Don't mention it.
I must apologize for being so late.

Introductions

Hello. My name's Peter. What's your name?
Janet.
Where are you from Janet?
I'm from Seattle. Where are you from?
I'm from Madrid.
Are you American?

CONVERSATIONS USING EXPRESSIONS

The Expressions have been written on the top. These are good to use in daily life.

CONVERSATION 1

I couldn't help it!!!

Rohan I am upset. Somebody told my boss I have a part-time job.

Raj And he doesn't like that?

Rohan No, he doesn't. He thinks that I am too tired to work.

Raj I am sorry. I have to admit I told him.

Rohan You told him? Why?

Raj **I couldn't help it**. He asked me **point-blank**.

> ***Explanation***: If you *can't help* the way you feel or behave, you cannot control it or stop it from happening. You can also say that you *can't help yourself*.
>
> If you say something *point-blank*, you say it very directly or rudely, without explaining or apologizing.

CONVERSATION 2

Everything went like clockwork!!!

Mr. Sharma I've just popped in to thank you very much for organizing last weekend's trip to the seaside for the old folk.

Mr. Singh That's very kind of you. They all seemed to enjoy it.

Mr. Sharma They certainly did. **Everything went like clockwork**, in fact I don't think you could have done it better.

Mr. Singh I'm not sure about that; there were one or two things that could have been improved.

Mr. Sharma In a perfect world perhaps, but as far as I'm concerned it was a great success. So thank you again.

> **Explanation**: If you say that something happens **like clockwork** you mean that it happens without any problems or delays, or happens regularly.

CONVERSATION 3

Don't be so pessimistic!

Priya That history exam was really awful. My worst so far.

Pooja Was it really so bad?

Priya Yes it was. Only a couple of the topics which I reviewed for the exam came up.

Pooja That was really bad luck. Do you think you managed to do enough to pass?

Priya No, I think I'll definitely fail that exam.

Pooja Oh, come on, **don't be so pessimistic.**

Explanation: *Pessimistic* - The feeling that bad things are more likely to happen than good things.

CONVERSATION 4

They'll need to check you out!!!

Shyam I heard that you're going for a new job.

Mohan Sure am. I've applied to be a Customer Care Executive at a call centre.

Shyam Why do you want to change? More money?

Mohan It's partly that, but I've got fed up with being a traveling salesman.

Shyam Is that the introduction page? It looks very long.

Mohan Yes, two pages. They want to know all about you.

Shyam And then **they'll need to check you out**. They'll probably use a specialist company to do that.

Mohan I know. It's a long process.

Explanation: **Check someone out** - Investigate or evaluate someone.

CONVERSATION 5

I have got a splitting headache!!!

Chavi Are you coming to the restaurant with us **Jyoti**?

Jyoti No, I'm sorry. I can't, **I've got a splitting headache.** I'm having one of my migraines.

Chavi Oh, you poor thing. Is there anything I can do?

Jyoti No, it's all right. I've taken my pills and I'll just stay in and lie down.

Chavi That's a miserable way to spend the day. Tell you what; I'll bring you some of your favourite pastries on my way home.

Jyoti That's very kind. It'll give me something to look forward to.

Explanation: Splitting headache/ pounding headache - Severe headache.

CONVERSATION 6

My mind suddenly went blank!!!

Gauri Now come on, calm down, it's not the end of the world. It was just an exam.

Mahima But it was absolutely awful. I just don't know why it happened.

Gauri Why what happened?

Mahima I'd just started on the third and last question when **my mind suddenly went blank.** I couldn't remember anything of what I'd reviewed for that topic.

Gauri But you answered the first two questions?

Mahima Well yes, but ...

Gauri Then stop worrying. I'm sure you did enough on those to pass.

Explanation: Your mind is a/goes blank - When **your mind is a blank/goes blank**, you cannot remember a particular thing, or you cannot remember anything.

CONVERSATION 7

Get it over with!!!

Seema Come on, let's go.

Shilpa I'm not going to enjoy this.

Seema Don't be such a misery, exercise is good for you.

Shilpa Going to the gym is not my idea of fun.

Seema But think what it'll do for your figure.

Shilpa OK, let's **get it over with** as fast as we can and then we'll have some real fun.

Explanation: Get it over (with) - Complete, have done with, especially something unpleasant.

Example: I might as well sign the check and **get it over with.**

CONVERSATION 8

The cut-off date is only two days away!!!

Henna There are so many different courses on offer on the course schedule.

Robin Yes, I'm finding it difficult to make up my mind which ones are the right ones for me.

Henna Maybe it would be best to get some advice from the student adviser.

Robin That's a good idea. I don't want to register for a course that turns out to be unsuitable.

Henna We'd better do that straight away, because we haven't got a lot of time.

Robin I know, **the cut-off date is only two days away.**

Explanation: Cut-off date - Deadline.

CONVERSATION 9

Take a photo of me!!!

Mahesh Excuse me, sorry to trouble you. Can you please **take a photo of me**?

Anish Of course. No problem. Where would you like me to take it?

Mahesh Just under the departures sign thanks.

Anish You look like you're going somewhere tropical. Where are you going?

Mahesh Oh, nowhere. I just want my friends to think that I can afford a great holiday. Thank you.

CONVERSATION 10

The dish is too hot!!!

Rita I'd like to order the special please.

Waiter I'm sorry you can't do that. **The dish is too hot.**

Rita Please don't tell me what I can or cannot eat. I love spicy food. I can eat it so bring me the special no matter how hot it is.

Waiter It's not spicy, I meant it's a hot item tonight and we've sold out. The special is unavailable.

Rita Ah, sorry.

CONVERSATION 11

Exceeding the speed limit.

Harish Just my luck. Look at this letter.

Jai Ah yes, I thought it was something official looking. You're being fined for **exceeding the speed limit** it says. Why weren't you fined on the spot?

Harish Because I was photographed by a speed camera. I didn't even know it was there.

Jai They're installing more and more of them around here. Two of my friends were caught speeding by them last month. You're going to have to be more careful in future.

Harish You're not kidding - the fine is Rs. 500. That's a lot of money and it would be double if I got caught again.

Jai I know, speeding is an expensive hobby.

CONVERSATION 12

Shell out a lot more money for extras!!!

Bobby Did you enjoy your theme park visit?

Vinay On the whole yes; there was certainly a lot to see and we had a very full day.

Bobby You don't sound totally enthusiastic.

Vinay Well that's because the entrance fee was quite high, but once inside we had to **shell out a lot more money for extras** which I think ought to have been included in the ticket price.

Bobby What sort of extras?

Vinay Well, for example, travelling between the different attractions on the electric bus. We had to pay for each separate journey.

Explanation: If you **shell out** for something, you spend a lot of money on it.

CONVERSATION 13

There was no give and take at all!!!

Paul That was a really hard negotiation.

Kate I can see; you look really exhausted. What was the problem?

Paul They were very inflexible and just stuck to their original position.

Kate So **there was no give-and-take at all.**

Paul No, none at all, because they knew they were in a very strong position.

Kate No wonder you had such a hard time.

CONVERSATION 14

You could do just as well!!!

Sanya: Those watercolours are really beautiful.

Priya: I'm glad you like them. I painted them last year.

Sanya You painted them yourself? I can't believe it, they're so good.

Priya: They're not that good, but I'm glad you like them.

Sanya: You're so talented; I wish I had your skill.

Priya: You should try your hand yourself; I'm sure **you could do just as well** if not better.

CONVERSATION 15

It's very temperamental!!!

Bobby Why has the photocopier stopped?

Leena Oh, it's probably because the paper has jammed. You'll have to open the door and look inside the machine to check.

Bobby Oh yes, I can see where a sheet of paper has got stuck.

Leena You need to follow the instructions printed inside the door to remove it and restart the machine.

Bobby That wasn't too difficult. Well, I'll restart the machine and hope for the best.

Leena You'll need a lot of hope for that machine. **It's very temperamental** and really needs replacing.

CONVERSATION 16

You have such good taste!!!

Monty: So this is your new apartment.

Sanya: Yes, I moved in a month ago.

Monty Well, I have to say it looks fantastic. Did you decorate and furnish it yourself.

Sanya Yes, I did. It took me quite a lot of time.

Monty Well, I must say you have such good taste in interior decor. A professional designer could have done it.

Sanya Oh! I don't think so, but I'm glad you think it's nice.

SOME OTHER CONVERSATIONS

1. ***Any time that you wish to speak to someone, first please say excuse me:***

> Student: "Excuse me sir?"
> Teacher: "Yes?"
> Student: "May I ask you something?"
> Teacher: "Yes, of course, what is your question?

2. ***If you do not hear what someone has said, you say:***

> Student: "Pardon, but I did not hear you. Can you say that again?"
> Teacher: "Yes, I said..."
> Student: "Thank you."
> Teacher: "You are welcome."

3. ***Or if you want SOMEONE to explain something again:***

> Student: "Excuse me sir, but can you explain that part again?"
> Teacher: "Yes, certainly. Which part?"
> Student: "Can you explain what pardon means?"
> Teacher: "Yes, pardon is used to ask someone to say that same thing again. Pardon is also used to say I am sorry, or excuse me. For sorry or excuse me, it is better to say; 'Pardon me.' Or, if you wish to pass by someone, say, 'Pardon me, can you let me pass?'"
> Student: "Thank you."
> Teacher: "You are welcome. Thank you for asking."

CONVERSATION BETWEEN THREE PEOPLE IN A CAFÉ

***Akira** and **Natasha** are sitting in a café*
Akira: Hi there!

Natasha: Hello.

Akira: What's your name?

Natasha: What's your name?

Akira: **Akira**. Where are you from?

Natasha: Russia. I'm a Russian.

Akira: I'm Japanese. I live in Osaka.

Natasha: I live in Moscow. I'm a student at Moscow University.

Akira: I'm a student too. I'm studying electronics.

Natasha: I'm studying computer science and English.

Akira: Do you like music?

Natasha: I don't understand.

Akira: Do you like music? (sings) La la la la...

Natasha: Uh yes. I love music. I play the piano.

Akira: I play the piano. I play the guitar, too, but I'm no good at it.

Natasha: I also play the violin. What music do you like?

Akira: I like lots of music. Bach and The Beatles.

Natasha: Me too. I like jazz and salsa. I like dancing.

Akira: You Russians are famous for dancing–I remember Rudolf Nureyev.

Natasha: Nureyev was a great dancer. I like ballet, but I prefer modern dance.

(A long-haired young man walks up to the table with a guitar. He is wearing hippie clothes. He plays the guitar to them. His name is ***Jimi****.)*

Jimi: Hi, guys. Can you spare some change?

Akira: Sit down. I'll buy you a drink.

Jimi: Hey, that's cool, man.

Natasha: What's you name?

Jimi: **Jimi**. Spelled J-I-M-I. Like Hendrix.

Natasha: I like **Jimi** Hendrix. He was a great guitarist.

Jimi: The greatest!

Akira: I like Segovia, too. There are many great guitarists.

Jimi: True, man. The world is full of good musicians.

Natasha: Were you born in San Francisco? I'm from Moscow, and **Akira** is from Osaka.

Jimi: No–I was born in Illinois–in a town 100 miles from Chicago.

Akira: What would you like to drink?

Jimi: I'll have a caffe latte. Can I have a Danish as well?

Akira: Yes, of course.

*(**Akira** signals to the waitress. She walks over and takes the order.)*

Natasha: How long have you lived in San Francisco?

Jimi: Seven years. It's a great city, but housing is expensive.

Akira: Housing is expensive in Osaka. Very expensive.

Natasha: Housing is a problem in big cities.

Jimi: Yeah – no problem in my hometown. Peoria, Illinois.

(The waitress brings the coffee and Danish pastry.)

Akira: How old are you, **Jimi**?

Jimi: Twenty-five. And you?

Akira: I'm twenty-two.

Natasha: I'm twenty-four.

Jimi: What are you guys doing in the States?

Akira: We're both studying. I'm studying electronics, and **Natasha** is studying English and computer science.

Jimi: Man, I hate computers. I like acoustic music and nature.

Natasha: I hate computers, too, and I like acoustic music and nature. But we need computers in the modern world.

Akira: Do you like sport?

Jimi: Sure – I love baseball. Tennis, too.

Akira: Do you like football?

Jimi: No – all those big, fat guys in helmets.

Akira: No, no – I mean the other football. You play with your feet.

Jimi: You mean soccer. I don't know anything about soccer.

Natasha: But soccer is the most popular game in the world!

Jimi: Maybe, – but not in the U.S. of A.

Akira: I love soccer *and* baseball. Sometimes I watch American Football.

Babe Ruth, Pele, Hank Aaron, Maradona – they're my heroes.

Natasha: American and English people don't like to learn other languages!

Akira: No! Everyone wants to speak English!

***Jimi** picks up his guitar again – he plays Here, There and Everywhere, by The Beatles. **Natasha** and **Akira** sing with him.*

Natasha: That was fun! Play another one.

Jimi: First I need another coffee.

Natasha:: No problem.

(She signals to the waitress.)

Akira: Do you know any Sting songs?

Jimi: Sure.

Jimi: My father is dead. He used to be an engineer. He was a civil engineer – he built roads and bridges.

Akira: I'm sorry he has died.

(Another girl Sheila joins them)

Jimi: He lived a good life, and he was a good father. I loved him very much.

Sheila: My father has a farm. He has lots of sheep. What about your dad, **Natasha**?

Natasha: My dad is a lorry driver.

Akira: What is a lorry?

Natasha: A truck. In England they say a "lorry", but in America they say a "truck".

Jimi: Yeah, the English talk a different language. (He laughs.)

Sheila: Well, in Australia we have different words. We say "bonzer" when we mean "excellent" or "very good". He have lots of slang words.

*(A waiter comes up to the table. They order drinks: coffees for **Akira** and **Natasha**, an orange juice for **Jimi** and a beer for **Sheila**.)*

Jimi: So you like beer, **Sheila**.

Sheila: All Australians like beer. It's our national drink.

Jimi: It's our national drink too!

Sheila: No, it's not. Your national drink is Coca-Cola.

Jimi: Yuggh! I hate Coca-Cola.

Akira: I like it, myself.

Natasha: Russia's national drink is vodka.

The others together: We know that!

Akira: Can I have a go on your guitar, **Jimi**?

Jimi: Sure.

*(**Jimi** hands **Akira** the guitar. **Akira** plays a classical piece.)*

Sheila: That's really nice, **Akira**. What is it called?

Akira: It's a piece by Bach – it's called Jesu, Joy of Man's Desiring.

Jimi: Cool sounds, man.

Natasha: I'd like to learn the guitar.

Jimi: It's not difficult to start. First you must buy a guitar.

*(New character: **Lee**, a local Chinese) A young man approaches them – he looks Chinese.*

Lee: Hey there, folks! What's happening?
Akira: Hi. We're just sitting around, playing some music and talking. Join us.
Lee: Cool. How do you people like San Francisco? You look like strangers.
Jimi: Yeah, man – I'm from Illinois.
Lee: Hey! I got a brother in Illinois. Cicero.
Jimi: Cicero! That's where Al Capone was a big-time gangster.
Lee: That's the one. My brother is a big-time geek.
Natasha: Geek? What's a geek?
Sheila: You know – a nerd, a computer nut. I use computers, but I don't know how they work inside.
Akira: You speak very fluent English. Were you born here?
Lee: Right on. San Francisco for at least five generations. My ancestors came over for the Gold Rush.
Akira: 1849.
Lee: The Forty-niners. Man, that must have been a crazy time!
Akira: What about the 1960s?
Lee: Too young, man. A big regret. My father had a ball, but he never tells me the details.
Sheila: My mother was here in the 1960s. She laughs about it when I ask her, but never tells me anything either.
Jimi: Shoot – wish I'd been there then.
Lee: Look on the bright side: we're still young!

(End of Conversation. They all go)

Shopping for a Sweater

Can I help you?
Yes, I'm looking for a sweater.
What size are you?
I'm an extra large.
How about this one?
Yes, that's nice. Can I try it on?
Certainly, there's the changing rooms over there.
Thank you.
How does it fit?
It's too large. Do you have a large?
Yes, here you are.
Thank you. I'll have it, please.
OK, how would you like to pay?
Do you take credit cards?
Yes, we do. Visa, Master Card and American Express.
OK, here's my Visa.
Thank you. Have a nice day!
Thank you, goodbye.

Personal Information

What's your surname (family name)?
Smith
What's your first name?
Fred
Where are you from?
Atlanta, Georgia
What's your job?
I'm a teacher.
What's your address?
34 White Street
What is your phone number?
308-6730
How old are you?
54
Are you married?
Yes, I am.

Common Vocabulary for Use

Some other Common words for using in everyday conversation with their meanings

bottom (n)
at the end.

common (adj)
you see it a lot.

conversation (n)
a talk with somcone.

correct (adj)
right NOT wrong.

drag (v)
to pull to another part

formal (adj)
if a word is formal, you say it to people who you do not know very well.

how many (question)
if you ask how many, you ask for a number.

introduce (v)
to put new people together.

know (v)
if you know something, you understand and believe it.

look (v)
if you look, you use your eyes to see things.

people (n)
many humans (irregular plural form of person).

phrases (n)
groups of words.

short (adj)
here, not long.

space (n)
a gap in the sentence.

ways (n)
different possibilities.

yourself (pronoun)
you.

birthday (n)
anniversary of the day on which a person was born.

click (v)
you press the button on your computer mouse to make a click.

height (n)
your height is how tall you are.

list (n)
a group of words in a line or column.

live (v)
to have one's home in a particular place.

married (adj)
if you are married, you have a wife or a husband.

movies (n)
'the movies' - cinema.

metre (n)
a unit of measurement. A metre is 100 centimetres.

rap (n)
a type of modern music.

salsa (n)
a type of music from South America.

single (adj)
if you are single, you are not married.

add up (v)
to add numbers together *e.g.* 2+2 = 4.

beat (v)
to win.

different (adj)
not the same.

differently (adv)
not doing it in the same way.

expensive (adj)
costing a lot of money.

in order (phrase)
in a correct line *e.g.* 1, 2, 3, 4 etc.

know (v)
here, to be friends with the person.

leaving (v)
to leave means to go away from.

left (v)
the past tense of 'to leave'.

parts (n)
a part is a bit of something.

PC (n)
a computer.

pronunciation (n)
the way you say something.

RAM (n)
memory in a computer.

rent (n)
money you pay to live in a house or flat that you do not own.

shirt (n)
men and women wear shirts on the top half of their bodies.

stress (n)
the 'loud' or accentuated part of a word.

was born (v)
'to be born' - when you came into the world.

above (prep)
over.

again (adv)
another time, or to repeat.

diagram (n)
a simple picture with lines.

different (adj)
another or not the same.

finishes (v)
to finish means to stop.

informal (adj)
not formal, something you say to friends.

lorry driver (n)
a person who drives a lorry (a large vehicle which carries things).

alarm clock (n)
makes a noise to wake us up in the morning.

certain (adj)
specific.

daily (adv)
every day.

distance (n)
the number of miles between two places.

dry (v)
to do something to stop it being wet.

dusting (v)
to remove dust from a house.

food (n)
things we eat.

hoovering (v)
to hoover the house or vacuum clean it with a machine.

housework (n)
work to make the house clean and tidy.

ironing (v)
what you do to shirts to make them look good after they are washed.

lawn (n)
the grass in front of or behind a house.

long (adj)
here, many miles.

make up (n)
things like lipstick which women put on their faces.

middle (n)
in the center.

teeth (n)
in our mouth, used for chewing.

tired (adj)
when you feel like sleeping.

mounts (n)
a quantity of something.

available (adj)
which you can get

company (n)
a business.

control (v)
to decide what to do with things.

dictate (v)
to speak and have what you say written down.

in real time (phrase)
at exactly the same time.

libraries (n)
places where you can borrow books. Do not confuse libraries with bookshops.

lose (v)
if you lose something, you cannot find it.

organise (v)
if you organise something, you put it in order or make it tidy.

quickest (adj)
fastest.

replaced (v)
to replace is to put in the place of another thing.

save (v)
to keep.

snail mail (n)
used to talk about letters sent by post.

spelling (n)
the way words are written.

take with (v)
it can go where you go.

type (v)
to write using a keyboard.

written (v)
past participle of 'to write'.

accident (n)
something bad that happens to you, for example, a car crash.

been (v)
past participle of 'to be'.

chance (n)
an opportunity to do something.

coach (n)
a vehicle which can carry about 50 people.

flight (n)
the journey on a plane.

handbag (n)
used by women to carry personal things in.

hotel (n)
a large building with many rooms in which people sleep.

lose (v)
if you lose something, you cannot find it.

send (v)
if you send something you post it, like a letter.

stolen (v)
past participle of "to steal" which means to take something from someone.

take with (v)
bring.

though (adv)
however.

unusual (adj)
strange, odd, or not normal or usual.

apartment (n)
a flat.

arrived (v)
if you arrive somewhere, you get to or reach your destination.

ate (v)
Past Simple of 'to eat'.

balcony (n)
the area in the open air which is outside a room in a hotel. You can sit on a balcony.

bill (n)
a piece of paper with the amount of money you have to pay written on it.

cleans (v)
you clean something when it is dirty.

complained (v)
if you complain, you have a problem which you want someone to help you with.

credit card (n)
a plastic card which you can use to pay for things.

dial (v)
to make a phone call.

free (adj)
for no money. It also means available or not occupied.

guests (n)
people who visit a hotel.

hairdryer (n)
an electrical appliance you use to make wet hair dry.

key (n)
you use a key to unlock a door.

luggage (n)
all your bags and suitcases.

midday meal (n)
the meal you eat in the middle of the day.

outside line (n)
a phone line which lets you call phones outside a hotel.

paid (v)
Past Simple of 'to pay'.

share (v)
if you share something, you and other people can use it.

suitable (adj)
corresponding to a need.

weekend (n)
Saturday and Sunday.

without charge (phrase)
you pay no money.

bilingual (adj)
in two languages.

bottom (n)
below at the end.

chat room (n)
a place on the world wide web where people chat to each other by writing.

check back (phrasal verb)
to look at again.

decide (v)
to choose between two ideas.

general (adj)
regular.

keep (v)
to save.

latest (adj)
most recent or newest.

magazines (n)
things to read, they are usually about one topic. *Vogue* is an example of a woman's magazine.

mind maps (n)
used as a way of learning things. In a mind map you do not write things in a list. You write or draw them inside circles across a page and make different connections between them.

monitor (n)
the screen where you can see your work on a PC.

repeat (v)
to do again.

video clips (n)
short video scenes.

web sites (n)
pages on the Internet.

avoid (v)
if you avoid something, you try not to see it or go near it.

badminton (n)
a game played on a court with a racket and a shuttlecock.

borrow (v)
if you borrow something, you have it for a short while but you must return it.

direction (n)
the direction of a movement is the position towards which you travel.

feed (v)
to give food to.

there is no point + verb + -ing (phrase)
if there is no point in doing something, then it is useless to do it.

lawnmower (n)
a machine used to cut grass.

level (n)
one floor of a building.

looks over (phrasal verb)
if something looks over something else, then it is higher than it.

soldiers (n)
a soldier is someone who works for the army.

store (v)
to hold and stock things before they are needed.

<u>tunnel</u> (n)
used for travelling under the ground.

zones (n)
a zone is an area which has a specific purpose.

back (n)
the area of your body between the shoulders and the bottom, which you can only see using a mirror.

Beefeaters (n)
The Beefeaters are men in red uniforms who guard the Tower of London.

circus acts (n)
the different kinds of shows you will see in a circus.

cool you down (phrase)
if something cools you down, it makes you feel less hot.

darker (adj)
if something is darker, it is blacker than anything else.

dry (adj)
opposite to *wet*.

escape (v)
if you escape from somewhere, you get out of an unpleasant place.

explains (v)
if you explain how to do something to someone, you tell them and help them.

get in (phrasal verb)
here, to enter.

hungry (adj)
if you are hungry, you need food.

Love (n)
feeling of liking someone.

models (n)
copies of things or people.

postcards (n)
you send postcards to people when you are on holiday. Postcards have pictures of places on the front of them.

protected (v)
if something is protected, no-one can hurt or damage it.

rides (n)
here, things such as big dippers which you find in themeparks.

rough (adj)
not smooth or flat.

scary (adj)
frightening.

seen (v)
past participle of 'to see'.

temporary (adj)
not permanent.

wild animals (n)
animals which are not pets.

accepted (v)
if you accept something, you say yes.

born (v)
when you are born you come into the world.

congratulations (exclamation)
this is said when you want to say *Well done* to someone.

dead (adj)
not alive or living.

found out (v)
past tense of 'to find' which means to discover some new information.

get on well with someone (phrasal verb)
to enjoy someone's company and have a lot to talk about.

immediately (adv)
at once.

marriage (n)
the act of getting married.

moved (v)
to move means to change the place where your live.

regularly (adv)
at equal spaces in time.

romance (n)
a love affair.

spent (v)
past tense of 'to spend', here, means passed time.

split up (phrasal verb)
if you split up from someone, you do not have a relationship with them anymore.

stages (n)
steps or periods of time.

status (n)
your status is your place in society.

wedding (n)
the event of getting married.

work out (phrasal verb)
if things do not work out, they go badly.

annoyed (adj)
if you are annoyed about something, you are angry about it.

character (n)
the kind of person you are.

cheerful (adj)
if you are cheerful, you are very happy.

danger (n)
something which will hurt you.

drawings (n)
pictures.

end (n)
the finish.

latest (adj)
here, most modern, fashionable.

manager (n)
the person who is at the top of a company.

marks (n)
the scores which your school work gets.

muscles (n)
the parts of your body which make you strong.

passes (v)
here, if you pass an exam, you do well in it.

scooter (n)
a two-wheel toy which you stand on and push along with a foot.

sports (n)
the general word for active games.

successful (adj)
if you are successful, you do very well at something.

sure (adj)
if you are sure, you are certain about something.

army (n)
the name for a large group of soldiers.

character (n)
a person in a movie. Actors and actresses play characters.

chases (v)
to chase is to go after someone and try to catch them.

clapped (v)
if you clap, you put your hands together to make a noise. You clap when you want to show how much you like something.

crashes (v)
if a car crashes, it hits something.

crime (n)
an action which is against the law.

dull (adj)
not interesting.

explosions (n)
an explosion is a blast which causes a lot of damage.

ghost (n)
ghosts are images of dead people which some people say they have seen for example, in old castles.

heart-warming (adj)
used to describe something which causes you to feel cheerful or happy.

hilarious (adj)
very funny.

in charge of (phrase)
means he is the boss.

involved (v)
if you are involved with something, you are part of it.

made me jump (phrase)
an action you make when you are suddenly frightened.

murder (n) and (v)
when someone gets killed by another person.

popular (adj)
a lot of people like it.

scandal (n)
a public problem of some kind.

space (n)
the area outside of the earth where all the other planets are.

spy (n)
a person who tries to steal secrets from another country.

stars (n) and (v)
with important actors / actresses in a film.

superb (adj)
very, very good.

translated (v)
if you translate language, you change it from one language to another.

behaviour (n)
the way in which people or animals act.

bombs (n)
things which make explosions.

captured (v)
if you are captured, a person holds you against your will.

carried out (phrasal verb)
to carry out means *to do*.

cocaine (n)
an illegal drug from South America.

copies (v)
to copy something is to make something which is exactly the same.

damaged (v)
to damage something is to change it for the worst.

deceiving (v)
if you deceive someone, you trick them.

downward (adj)
if something goes downward, it goes down.

exceptions (n)
an exception is something which does not fit the normal pattern.

factory (n)
a building where things like cars are made.

gain (v)
if you gain something, you get it.

genuine (adj)
a thing which is genuine is real and not fake.

held (v)
here, if you are held, you are kept prisoner. Past tense of 'to hold'.

heroin (n)
an illegal drug made from poppies.

hurt (adj)
if you are hurt, you feel pain.

inappropriate (adj)
if something is inappropriate, it is not used for its intended purpose.

increased (v)
to increase something means produce more of it.

infringe (v)
when you infringe something, you go against the law.

law (n)
the word for the legal system of a country.

level (n)
here, an amount.

middle class (n)
middle class people have salaries which are not high and not low, for example, teachers are middle class.

minor (adj)
if a crime is minor, it is not very important.

national (adj)
if something is national, it applies to all the country.

overall (adj)
the total.

overestimate (v)
if you estimate, you make a guess and so if you overestimate, your guess is too high.

pilot (n)
a person who flies a plane.

rate (n)
the rate at which something happens is the amount of it in a given time.

reasons (n)
a reason for doing something is why it is being done.

results (n)
the results of an action are what you see or have at the end of it.

seemed (v)
if something seems to do something, it appears to do it.

speed limit (phrase)
how fast you can drive on certain roads. For example, the speed limit on UK motorways is 70 mph.

survey (n)
a large piece of research which collects information and presents the results.

taken over (v)
here, to take over means *to take control*.

trend (n)
a pattern.

vehicles (n)
this is the word for all forms of transport.

accompany (v)
to accompany something means go with it.

bass guitar (n)
a guitar which plays low sounds. It has 4 strings.

broadsheet (n)
large format English newspaper.

burning (v)
when a thing is burning it is on fire.

chew (v)
to move our teeth up and down when food is in our mouth.

disapprove (v)
if you disapprove of something, you do not agree with it.

essays (n)
an essay is a piece of writing done by a student.

going off (phrasal verb)
here, if a bomb goes off, it explodes.

guessed (v)
if you guess, you make an attempt but you are not sure you are correct.

intake (n)
something which is taken in. Here, air into your mouth.

itch (v)
a small tickle on our skin which makes us feel as if we want to scratch it.

musical instrument (n)
a thing you can play music on like a guitar or a piano.

newborn (adj)
a newborn animal or human is a very young one which has only been alive a short while.

noticed (v)
if you notice something, you see it by accident.

pedestrian (n)
someone walking in a street.

perfectly (adv)
here, very.

realised (v)
when you realise something, you come to know it is true.

runny (adj)
full of water. This is often used for noses.

set the clock (phrase)
to use the buttons on the clock to make it ring at a special time.

sharp (adj)
very quick.

squeaky (adj)
has a high-pitched sound.

still (adj)
here, not moving.

that's strange (phrase)
you say this when something is unusual.

usual (adj)
normal.

aches (n)
an ache is a pain in any part of the body.

bacteria (n)
tiny organisms which live in the air.

cells (n)
a cell is the smallest part of a living being which can live all by itself.

come into contact with (phrase)
meet.

expecting (v)
if you expect something, you think it will happen.

extremely (adv)
very.

germ (n)
a very, very, small living thing which causes illness. Germs live in humans, animals and food.

immediately (adv)
very quickly.

joints (n)
parts of the body between different bones.

negative (adj)
here, thinking that bad things will happen.

newly (adv)
recently.

nod (v)
we nod when we say yes. Our head goes up and down.

organ (n)
here, an internal part of the body.

performed (v)
here, carried out.

prevent (v)
to stop something happening.

replaced (v)
to change for another one of the same kind.

second-hand (adj)
already used.

section (n)
a section of a building is a special area in it.

severe (adj)
very bad.

spots (n)
small, red and sometimes painful areas of skin.

sudden (adj)
quickly without warning.

accomplished (adj)
very talented.

aerosol (n)
used to spray the contents of a can.

bad breath (phrase)
when a person's breath has a bad smell.

bandaged up (v)
to cover a part of your body that has been hurt in some cloth (or a special bandage).

boulder (n)
a big piece of rock.

briefly (adv)
for a short period of time.

carried out (phrasal verb)
if something is carried out, it is done and completed.

curry (n)
type of food from countries such as India. It is usually hot and spicy.

distinguishing (adj)
has special features which help you know one thing from another of the same type.

go mountain biking (v)
popular sport with a special bicycle for riding off the roads on rough ground.

idiomatic (adj)
informal language.

intend to (v)
if you intend to do something, you have a plan to do it.

overhead (adj)
above people's heads or high up in the sky.

printed (v)
to print is to put words or pictures onto paper from a machine such as a computer.

reporters (n)
another word for journalists.

run out of (phrasal verb)
you have no more of something.

surface (n)
flat area.

trapped (v)
if you are trapped, you cannot move or escape.

ugh (exclamation)
this is an expression which means *I do not like this*.

unusual (adj)
not usual, or strange and odd.

armed (adj)
if a person is armed, they have a weapon such as a gun.

attend (v.)
here, go to.

case (n)
here, the crime.

considering (v)
when people consider something, they think about it for a short period of time.

counter (n)
the part of a bank or shop which separates the customers from the employees, like a high table top.

demanded (v)
if people demand something, they say you must do it.

expert (n)
a person who knows a lot about a specific subject.

investigation (n)
the process of trying to find out about something.

originally (adv)
here, at the start.

prove (v)
when you prove something, you show how it is done and use things to demonstrate this.

raided (v)
when a bank is raided, it is attacked.

recovered (v)
found.

responsible (adj)
here, the person who did something.

scarf (n)
a piece of clothing which you put around your neck in the winter.

solve (v)
to find the answer to a problem.

suspected (v)
if a person is suspected of doing something, police believe they did it.

taken place (phrase)
when an event takes place, it happens.

truth (n)
uncountable noun, opposite of *lies*.

wrapped (v)
to wrap something means *to cover it*.

bones (n)
our bones are hard, white material inside our bodies.

break out (phrasal verb)
here, to start.

camels (n)
large, beige animals with humps on their backs.

collision (n)
when two things knock into each other.

define (v)
if you define something, you give a clear and exact description of it.

destruction (n)
the process of destroying something.

drop (n)
here, a fall or a vertical surface.

drown (v)
to die in water.

flows (v)
moves in a direction.

mixture (n)
when two or more things have been put together. For example, a mixture of eggs, milk and butter is used to make omelettes.

molten (adj)
not solid, melted with heat.

remains (n)
what is left over.

ski-slopes (phrase)
the places on a mountain where people ski.

sticky (adj)
describes thing in glue form.

suck (v)
to pull in one direction.

sunk (v)
past participle of 'to sink' which means go under the water.

tankers (n)
very large ships used to carry oil.

warns (v)
tells someone of a possible danger.

alter (v)
to change a state in some way.

chain (n)
a series.

chef (n)
a person whose job is to cook.

chilli (adj or n)
red powder which makes food hot and spicy.

cumin (n)
a yellow spice.

expert (n)
a person with special skills or knowledge.

fibre (n)
food from plants which is good for your health because it passes through your digestive system quickly.

ingredients (n)
all the items which are used to cook a specific dish.

layering (v)
to put into layers.

portions (n)
a quantity which is enough for one person.

refined (adj)
of a high quality.

salsa (n)
sauce.

seeded (adj)
has the seeds taken out.

set on fire (phrase)
to light with matches.

sour (adj)
the opposite of *sweet*.

spicy (adj)
has a hot taste.

sprinkle (v)
to spread powder.

squash (v)
to change something from a solid state to a near liquid state.

strands (n)
a strand is a small thin strip of something.

tortilla (n)
Mexican pancake made of flour.

whole wheat (phrase)
made with wheat which is not crushed.

approach (v)
to go near to something.

ceases (v)
finishes.

combination (n)
things which are put together.

commits crimes (phrase)
to do things which are against the law.

conscientious (adj)
very thorough, organised and hard-working.

dedicated (adj)
devoted and loyal.

disappointed (adj)
the feeling when you are let down.

disillusioned (adj)
the feeling you have when things are not what you expected them to be.

distinguished (adj)
successfully achieved many things.

down-trodden (adj)
oppressed by other people.

dysfunctional (adj)
do not work together well.

eventually (adv)
in the end.

for a change (phrase)
to be different than usual.

honour (n)
the feeling when you are very proud to be chosen to do something.

permission (n)
agreement from someone.

potential (n)
talent to be developed.

rear (v)
raise children.

represents (v)
symbolises.

sensible (adj)
does the correct thing.

steeply (adv)
going up at a fast rate.

stick together (phrasal verb)
unite.

anatomy (n)
the study of the human body.

anthropology (n)
the study of the evolution of different societies.

biological (adj)
of living things.

broth (n)
an old word for soup which is not generally used now.

degree (n)
the award you get when you finish university.

development (n)
the way things grow and change over a period of time.

Dr (abbreviation)
this is short for Doctor.

forcefully (adv)
done with strength and force.

humanities (n)
the study of the range of subjects concerned with humans and the way we live.

outline (n)
a short description.

perspectives (n)
different ways of looking at the same thing.

physiology (n)
the study of the way a living thing works.

subjects (n)
areas which we study such as Maths.

swarm (n)
a large group of bees.

whales (n)
very large animals which live in the sea. Some species of whale are nearly extinct.

ll the time (phrase)
continuously.

character (n)
a letter on a PC keyboard or on a mobile phone.

chat rooms (n)
places on the Internet where people talk to each other with written text.

evolved (v)
if something evolves, it grows at a natural speed.

fixed (adj)
stable, or does not move.

intimately (adv)
is known very well.

keypads (n)
places on a keyboard or a mobile phone where you touch to write letters.

phenomenal (adj)
very dramatic.

popularity (n)
when a thing or person is very much liked by others.
serve (v)
be of a useful purpose.

surprising (adj)
makes you surprised, or get unexpected information.

uncovered (v)
found out or discovered.

Other Books on

WORD POWER SERIES

1. Effective English Comprehension Read Fast, Understand Better ! **(New)**
2. Latest Essays for College & Competitive Examinations **(New)**
3. Dictionary of New Words **(New)**
4. Art of English Conversation Speak English Fluently **(New)**
5. Teach Yourself English Grammar & Composition **(New)**
6. Common & Uncommon Proverbs **(New)**
7. Effective Editing Help Yourself in Becoming a Good Editor **(New)**
8. Effective English A Boon for Learners **(New)**
9. Essays for Primary Classes
10. Essays for Junior Classes
11. Essays for Senior Classes
12. Dictionary of Synonyms and Antonyms
13. Dictionary of Idioms and Phrases
14. Common Phrases
15. How to Write & Speak Correct English
16. Meaningful Quotes
17. Punctuation Book
18. Top School Essays
19. How to Write Business Letters with CD
20. Everyday Grammar
21. Everyday Conversation
22. Letters for All Occasions

23. School Essays & Letters for Juniors
24. Common Mistakes in English
25. The Power of Writing
26. Learn English in 21 Lessons
27. First English Dictionary
28. Boost Your Spelling Power
29. Self-Help to English Conversation
30. The Art of Effective Communication
31. A Book of Proverbs & Quotations
32. Word Power Made Easy
33. English Grammar Easier Way
34. General English for Competitive Examinations
35. Spoken English
36. School Essays, Letters Writing and Phrases
37. How to Write & Speak Better English
38. Quote Unquote (A Handbook of Famous Quotations)
39. Improve Your Vocabulary
40. Common Errors in English
41. The Art of Effective Letter Writing
42. Synonyms & Antonyms
43. Idioms
44. Business Letters

Unit No. 220, Second Floor, 4735/22,
Prakash Deep Building, Ansari Road, Darya Ganj,
New Delhi - 110002, Ph.: 32903912, 23280047, 09811594448
E-mail: lotus_press@sify.com, www.lotuspress.co.in